The S⟮

"If you're brave enough to say goodbye,
life will reward you with a new hello."
- Paulo Coehlo

"Never love anybody that
treats you like you're ordinary"
- Oscar Wilde

"Bless those who walk away from you;
they are making room for those who won't."
- Unknown

"In the process of letting go, you will lose many
things from the past, but you will find yourself."
- Deepak Chopra

"Remember that sometimes not getting
what you want is a wonderful stroke of luck."
- Dalai Lam

"Pain is inevitable. Suffering is optional."
- M. Kathleen Casey

"Sara is the real deal. I have found not only comfort and wisdom in her words, but I have often shared her words with others."

- David

"The book *The Split* had answers I didn't even know I was searching for."

- Kate

"I've been bankrupt—even lost loved ones—but nothing was harder than divorce…and nothing helped more than this book."

- Jenifer

"This book is better than medication."

-Allie

"The only thing better than this book is working with Sara one on one; but if you can't do that, take advantage of every word on every page. It's a lifesaver."

- Tanya

The Split

The Split

From Breakup
to Breakthrough
in 30 Days or Less

Sara Davison

Speaker House Publishing

Dedication

For my parents,
who are my inspiration every day that true love exists

and for my gorgeous boy,
who I love so much for being him, just the way he is,
always and forever.

Special Thanks

I would like to say a special thank you to the people that have
been a constant source of support for me over the years. I
believe that the quality of your life is directly determined by the
quality of people you surround yourself with. And I am so
grateful to have all these people in my life.

My parents who are my rock and are always there for me and
my son. I'm so grateful for everything they do.

Santi for making me smile and laugh every day and for
reminding me what is most important in life. And for inspiring
me in so many ways to do the work that I do.

My brother Paul, for always being there and for his advice and constant support.

David Fagan for seeing the potential in me and making this book a reality. It's been so much fun working with him and his team.

Daniel Klayton for the hours we have spent talking about this book and for weaving his magic throughout.

Hayley Hamburg, my PR Agent, who is a joy to work with and has huge talent for creating incredible opportunities.

Becca Barr, my TV Agent and also my good friend, who inspires me with her intuition and spot on advice.

Brian and Janice for their incredible support and advice in growing my business online.

Bridgette, my fabulous PA, for helping support me and my clients at retreats and speaking events.

Jai and Sian, my amazing designers, who keep my brand on track with their creative genius.

Suze at Coathanger, my friend and stylist with an incredible eye for the perfect outfit.

Charlotte, my best friend since I was 10 years old, and a very special person in my life.

Sue for adding lots of sparkle to my life and being the sister I never had. And for all the weekends my son and I have spent with her beautiful family, it's our home away from home.

Lucy who has been such a wonderful friend to me and her son Max who is a great friend to Santi.

Simon who is an amazing friend and always there for me.

Beverley, Aaron and Cameron who are great fun and who my son and I love spending time with.

Victoria for being the best neighbor in the world and for appearing in her PJ's at 2am

Graeme, my personal trainer for 3 years, who always brightens up my day.

Graeme, my osteopath, who has no idea how much his support and advice has meant to me over the last few years.

Chrissie who has been such an incredible support in my recent journey. And for being an inspiration for me in so many ways.

All my clients for trusting in me and for being such a wonderful group of people. And for making my work so enjoyable and rewarding.

The whole team at The Dash Charity for all the amazing work they do for vulnerable women, children and men suffering from domestic abuse. And for the honor of inviting me to be their Patron.

I am so lucky to have you all in my life. Thank you!

Table of Contents

Introduction

When I opened the drawer that fateful morning and saw the contact-lens box staring up at me, I could just about feel my marriage, my family, everything I had built in my life, come crashing down around me.

Neither my husband nor I wore contacts, but there it was—a contact-lens box and the fake eyelash sitting on top of it, winking up at me in cruel mockery of my marriage. They were definitely not mine.

I couldn't avoid it any longer. Was my husband having an affair?

Sure, there had been warning signs and red flags before that morning, but like so many of us, I rationalized and reasoned my way around them; because there was no way—*no way*—that this was happening to me. From the outside I had a picture-perfect marriage and it just wasn't possible that my husband was secretly cheating.

But with that little contact-lens box and fake eyelash, everything changed.

Over the next months and years, I went through the pain and trauma of divorce. I was shocked by how utterly devastating the experience was—and there's a good chance you know exactly what I'm talking about.

The breakup of a relationship has been described as the second most traumatic life experience, only behind the death of a close loved one, and that was true for me. I was shocked that, even with my years of experience in coaching and personal development, and with therapists and loving friends and family on my team, I felt so shattered and lost.

I felt like something was missing.

I was longing for strategies to deal with the specific trauma of breakup, longing for a guide for this torturous new path I was walking; something that would show me the way to go, someone that would speak to me with both practical advice and compassionate understanding; something beyond empty platitudes like, "You'll get over this eventually!" or "You'll be happy again!" I wanted more concrete strategies and guidance, but I couldn't find any.

So, I decided to create it. And that's the book you're holding in your hands right now.

I've been a coach now for two decades, and for the last six years I've specialized as a divorce coach, dedicating myself to guiding others through breakup and divorce. I've helped thousands of clients work their way through the rocky terrain of breakup, empowering them to navigate the road from breakup to breakthrough.

Let's be clear here; this book isn't just for people going through divorce. Everything in these pages—all the tools, techniques, and strategies I'll give you apply to any kind of split. Maybe you're just into your twenties and grieving over the loss of your first love. Maybe you're facing the end of a decades-long marriage. Maybe you're tired of a pattern of broken relationships and ready for reinvention. Whatever your own situation might be, this book is for you.

This book is also for people from all walks of life. Women and men, TV stars and stay-at-home parents, young and old—all of us experience the heartbreak of a split at some point in our lives. The tools in this book to turn breakup into breakthrough will work for anyone.

That's the journey here: not just healing from a split, but turning that into life-changing breakthroughs.

If there's one thing I've learned through my years of work and my own experiences, it's that no matter how devastating a breakup can feel in the moment, it can also be a moment of life-changing transformation.

A split is a golden opportunity; it can lead you to a more fabulous and fulfilling life than you ever imagined possible.

I know that if you're holding this book in your hands right now, that might sound ludicrous. If you've picked up this book, odds are you're somewhere in the journey of a breakup. Maybe the split hasn't happened yet, maybe it has, but either way, the odds are that you're experiencing the pain and trauma of a relationship pulling apart.

That trauma can feel like a raging fire, consuming the life you had, the relationship you've been in for months, years, or even decades. I know how that fire can feel irreversibly destructive, and it's ok if you feel that way now.

I promise you, though; from the ashes of those flames, your new life will take flight, like a phoenix reborn; and when you dive into that transformative potential, your new life will be even more wonderful than you've dreamed possible. That might seem impossible to you right now—and that's ok because this book is your guide on that path, and I'll walk with you on that journey step by step. In these pages, we'll walk through my 30-day plan together to transform breakup into breakthrough.

For each day of this journey, I'll share with you the insights I've gained over years of work in this field, giving you strategies you need to move forward into a transformed future; and you won't just be reading about it; at every step, I'll be giving you tools and techniques to put this into practice right now.

There is no magic wand to take away all the pain of a split. I'm not going to promise you that 30 days from now you'll be completely over things, or that there won't be any more pain. If I could magically take the pain away, trust me, I would, but life just doesn't work that way.

Even though there isn't a magic wand, there *is* a remote control—the remote control to your mind; that's a tool I can give you, and I'll show you how to use it to start dialing down your pain. If your pain is at a 10 now, I'll show you how to dial that down to, say, a 7 or a 6, which can mean the difference between spending all day in bed, or pulling yourself up and starting to live your life again. Day by day, you'll learn new strategies to put yourself in the driver's seat of your emotions and steer yourself in the direction of happiness, passion, and excitement for an amazing future.

I can't promise you that everything will be perfect overnight, but what I can promise you is that if you join me on this journey and commit yourself fully, you'll be astonished 30 days from now at how far you've come. Where you feel helpless now, you'll feel empowered. Where you see only failure now, you'll see a world of rich possibilities. Where you're consumed by pain and despair now, you'll feel optimistic excitement—yes, genuine excitement—for what's ahead.

The next 30 days will be full of insights about yourself, inner transformation, and breakthrough. I'll guide you through taking stock of the big picture, healing the pain of your breakup, getting your life back on track, and moving into a fabulous new future of your design.

When I first saw that contact-lens box and fake eyelash staring at me, I could only see a crumbling marriage and despair. But looking back on it now, I see that moment as a pivotal step towards the wonderful, fulfilling life I'm living now. My life today isn't wonderful *despite* my divorce; it's wonderful *because of* the breakthroughs and transformation that my divorce opened up.

That's what's possible for you too. That's the beautiful, empowered life you deserve.

So, let's take our next step together and dive in.

Day 1:

Committing to Play Full-Out

Imagine that you have a goal of losing a few pounds and building your strength, so you decide to go out and join that gym down the street.

You really want to fit into that great summer outfit sitting in your closet, so every morning you wake up a couple hours early to go to the gym before work. You jump out of bed at the first alarm, grab your gym bag, and head out the door.

Every morning at the gym, you take a nice leisurely stroll through the various machines, but never actually use one. You walk by the treadmills, read all the instructions, and play with the controls so you know exactly how the machine works. You could be a certified expert in how to use it, but you never actually hop on and start running.

Are you going to lose those pounds?

Of course not!

When it comes to training and developing your physical body, you could have all the memberships to the best gyms and yoga studios, and all the best nutritional information, but if you don't dive in and do the work, you won't see the results you want. The very same is true when it comes to your inner transformation.

Remember, there is no magic wand that can instantly take away all your pain, and I can't do the work for you, but I am going to give you that remote control for your mind. I am going to fill your toolkit with strategies and techniques for dialing down the pain of heartbreak and dialing up the passion and excitement for the fabulous life ahead of you.

Even with all the best tools in your toolkit, though, it's your commitment to *putting them in action* that is going to make the difference, so right now, you're at a choice point.

I'm not just inviting you to the gym; I'm inviting you to hop up on the treadmills with me and start running!

Right here, you get to make the choice to commit. You're committing to play full out 100%; committing to put the work in to create the healing and breakthrough that you deserve.

Part of playing full out is doing the work even when you might not want to, in those moments when all you want to do is grab a huge bag of chips and bury yourself in bed all day. Maybe it'll be after you drop your child off with your ex and his new 22-year old girlfriend, or maybe after you're hit with a memory of the good times and it feels like your heart is breaking all over again.

Those moments—the really tough moments—are precisely when you get to pull out your new tools and put them to use. It's just like being at the gym. When you're on a weight machine, it's that last repetition—when your muscles are burning and you feel like you can't but you push through anyway—that builds the most strength.

So, when the going gets tough, and all you want to do is lie in bed and eat chips forever, that's when the real work gets going.

Does that mean that you need to get things perfectly right all the time, every time? No, of course not; this is a journey, and it's all about building experience and learning step by step how to better use that remote control for your mind. This is about committing to dive in and do your best.

Playing 100% also means trust—not just trusting that the tools I'm going to share with you will work—the results when you use them will be proof enough of that; you need to trust that things will get better *for you*.

When you're right in the stormy turmoil of a split, it can sometimes feel like it's impossible for things to ever get better. The sun will never shine like it used to, and passion, fun, and head-over-heels love are gone for good; trust me, I know how that feels, but it's vital that you trust that things *will* turn around for you, and that the life ahead of you will be even more fabulous than you could imagine. It's ok if you can't yet see the path that will lead you there. I'll be right here with you, guiding you through the next 30 days of breakthrough. At this point, all I'm asking is that you trust that the journey will work for *you*.

Are you ready to play this all-in game of breakthrough?

Ready to join me on this journey, heal the pain you might be feeling now, and write the next outrageously amazing chapter of your life?

Let's start putting it into action.

Make the commitment to yourself here and now, and sign below to commit to play full out and do what it takes to break through.

I, _____, am fully committed to diving in, playing full out, and making the most of the next 30 days of breakthrough.

Signature: _____

Date: _____

Day 2:

Your Breakthrough Journal

As we begin this journey together, you're going to start one of the most essential tools to use throughout this book: your breakthrough journal.

Your breakthrough journal is going to be your training field; your first playground to put all the strategies and techniques here into practice. Like so many of the tools you're going to discover throughout these next few weeks, the breakthrough journal is a simple one.

All you'll need is to get a blank journal to use throughout the book. It could be a composition notebook—one of those black-and-white marbled notebooks we all remember from school, a spiral notebook, a small moleskin that can fit in your pocket—whatever works best for you.

Like so many of the other simple tools you're going to discover throughout these pages, a breakthrough journal is absolutely essential.

Now, some of you might be thinking, "Well, getting a notebook probably means I'm going to actually have to *do* some of these exercises, which seems like a lot of work. Maybe I'll just read through the book first and do things on my own, and then perhaps get a journal later."

But remember what you committed to just yesterday!

You gave your word—to yourself, most importantly—that you were going to play full out throughout this journey.

Creating a breakthrough journal is an essential step in playing 100% full out.

Imagine if this were a book all about physical fitness, filled with golden strategies and breakthrough techniques for you to get stronger, lose weight, and build muscle tone. If you just read the book, maybe even read the book *really closely*, but never actually stepped into the gym and *did* the exercises and techniques that the book put forward, do you think you'd lose weight? If all you did was read it, do you think you'd build muscle and tone your body?

Of course not.

The same truth applies here, as together you and I transform the pain of a breakup into the life-changing power of breakthrough. For everything here to work, you get to put it to work *for you*!

Your breakthrough journal is that first playground where you'll start practicing.

Throughout the rest of this book, each day you'll find exercises and techniques for dialing down your pain, dialing up your passion and excitement and optimism, and creating breakthrough in your life. In almost every chapter, those exercises will first entail you to put things down on paper by practicing them in your breakthrough journal.

The ideal breakthrough journal for you will be one that you can keep on you or close to you all day. That might mean something that can fit in your pocket or purse, or it might be one that you'll keep in your backpack or briefcase. Physically keeping your journal near you will help you to stay connected to the work we're doing here and also make it easier for you to start putting these tools into practice in your everyday life.

As we move into later weeks and start focusing on goal-setting and creating the compelling future that rockets you forward, your breakthrough journal will also be the place where you track your progress towards individual goals, creating accountability, and ensuring you hit your targets.

As you train your breakthrough muscles and put these strategies into action day after day, your breakthrough journal will also be a tool to see for yourself how far you've come. At various points over the next few weeks, part of your journey will be to record how you're feeling and where your life is at that moment.

We'll use your breakthrough journal to gauge your progress, so it's important that whenever you work in it, you write down the date!

At the end of these 30 days, your breakthrough journal will be the tangible testament to your own progress. You'll be able to flip back through the pages to see how far you've come in such a short time; how much you've been able to dial down your pain and heartache; and how far you've dialed up your joy and passion and excitement. This view of your progress will cement the power of these tools and strategies, giving you the motivation to keep practicing throughout and beyond these 30 days.

Plus, that progress will be something to celebrate, and a huge part of turning a breakup into breakthrough is celebrating each step forward!

So, your assignment today is a simple one: get yourself a breakthrough journal. With that journal in hand, get ready to put the rubber to the road and rocket forward into your breakthrough life!

Day 3:

Laying the Groundwork for Breakthrough

At this point, you know I don't want you to just survive your breakup—I want to help you use it as a launch pad to take off into your new, transformed life. This book isn't about surviving; it's about thriving.

This is what really sets this book—the strategies, techniques, and tools I'm giving you—apart from other books about breakup or divorce. It's everything I wish I'd had access to during my own difficult breakup. I've tried and tested all these tools myself; I know they work because they worked for me.

Many books out there will give you some flowery talk about getting through things without actually giving you tangible tools to use. Others will give you a few really surface-level tools, but no momentum to move forward. If this is all you have, you're not going to create anything other than short-lived, surface-level results.

That's not what this book is about.

Over the course of these 30 days, we're going to dive deep together. The insights and self-awareness I'll guide you into and the techniques and strategies I'll be teaching you are ones that will go right to the core of who you are, how you live life, and how you relate to the people around you.

When we turn breakup into breakthrough, those breakthroughs aren't just about relationships.

Will they show up in how you approach dating and romance, and the sorts of relationships you build? Yes, of course! But they're also going to show up everywhere else in your life.

I know that might sound odd at first. How would working through a split have any impact on, say, your career? But let's look a little closer.

Maybe through the course of these 30 days, you'll uncover some issues with your personal confidence, seeing how a lack of confidence causes breakdowns in your romantic relationships. If that's the case, you'll start using the tools I give you to build and develop that confidence.

Now, imagine—if you start living life with a whole new level of confidence and belief in yourself, is it possible that's going to affect how you show up to your coworkers, or how you perform in your career? Absolutely!

Or to take another example, perhaps we'll uncover some issues you have with self-sabotage. If you're unconsciously sabotaging your romantic relationships, do you think it's possible you're also doing that with, say, your health and physical wellness? If you break that cycle of self-sabotage when it comes to romantic relationships, do you think you might also start breaking that cycle elsewhere? You bet.

Everyone has his or her own journey ahead, so you'll uncover your own personal insights and create your own unique breakthroughs, but I can guarantee that whatever insights and breakthroughs you do unleash, they're going to transform every area of your life.

A huge part of what makes this deep breakthrough possible is how we're going to illuminate something that drives your life without you even realizing it—your map of the world.

Your Map of the World

Everyone lives life with their own unique map of the world.

That map outlines how we think the world works, how interacting with other people should look, how we think about ourselves, and so on.

How should you handle an argument with a romantic partner? Letting all the emotions out in a loud shouting match? Or stepping away to cool off, until you can talk things over calmly? Your map of the world tells you what to do.

What does it look like to really show someone love? Words of affection and encouragement? Little gifts that show you care? Spending quality time together? Physical touch? Again, your map of the world tells you how important and meaningful each of those is.

Are people fundamentally trustworthy or does someone have to prove he or she can be trusted before you open up? Your map of the world tells you.

Are you worthy of a happy relationship, or are you destined for conflict and heartache? Again, your map of the world.

This map is what creates all the patterns you run unconsciously. For better and for worse, it's these patterns that create the results we have in life—both the good ones and the not-so-good ones.

Part of what makes relationships such a fraught adventure is that no two people have the exact same map of the world. We all interpret the world and filter our experiences differently.

Our individual maps are shaped by the people who most influenced us as young children. For the majority of us, those are our parents—either one or both of them. It might also be shaped by siblings, other relatives, or anyone else who had a profound impact on us as young children. These are the people who teach us how to see the world and who give us the patterns we run.

Our map of the world is also shaped by the politics we encounter, religions we're exposed to, monumental events, and experiences in our lives; all these teach us unconscious strategies and assumptions about the world and how to live in it.

Usually, all this is operating on an unconscious level. Just like a fish that never realizes it's in water because that's all it's ever known, we tend to use our own map of the world without ever realizing it. It's just the way things are.

My job is to help you become conscious of the patterns you're running. Together, you and I are going to bring the unconscious up into your conscious awareness. With that awareness, you'll be able to see what works and what doesn't work, empowering you to make new choices where you want to. When it's still buried in your unconscious, your map of the world shapes your life without you ever realizing it, but when you've become aware of it and you have the right tools, you can change it however you want; this, in turn, transforms your life.

We'll break this down deeper in later sections of this book, but for now, as we move into dealing with the immediate effects of your breakup, it's vital that you keep this big-picture concept in mind. For now, what I want you to think about is who you think you learned your map of the world from. Who or what had the most profound impact on you growing up?

Pull out your breakthrough journal and write a few pages about what has shaped your map of the world. Don't worry about getting all the perfect answers; for today, I want you to focus on just starting to think about your life in this way. You can just free-write about it and see what comes up.

Answering those questions will start to shine a light on your own unconscious patterns, and as we move into dealing with the immediate turmoil of your split, that light is going to start illuminating your way forward.

Day 4:

How Would You Describe Your Split Now?

To get started, we need to understand where you are right now in your breakup.

When I say *where you are*, I'm referring to your internal experience—what emotions you're experiencing and how intensely you're experiencing them. Every split is different, and everyone experiences their own split uniquely, so it's vital to understand clearly what it is that you're feeling right now.

I know that you might feel hesitant about looking closely at where you are in your split. It's often not so pleasant to look at, and it's natural to want to just avoid it, but clarity gives you power—we're going to talk more about that concept tomorrow—and my job is to give you your power back. Even if you don't like what you discover here—and it's ok if you don't—this process is going to empower you to turn your life around.

Oftentimes, the emotional chaos of a split can have us just feel overwhelmed with painful feelings.

When I ask clients to start describing how they're feeling, sometimes they'll go straight to descriptions like 'awful,' or 'terrible,' or 'like I just can't deal with this.' All of that is understandable, but to move forward we need to start discerning what is behind that, and what specifically is going on for you.

When you go to a doctor, you might start by saying, "I don't feel well." That's a starting point, but if you want to get well, you and your doctor will dig deeper into more specifics. Your doctor will work with you, asking questions to uncover what exactly is going on, so that you can start a plan to get well again.

That's the same sort of process we're going to take on here.

You might say that you're feeling awful about your split. Does feeling awful mean you're feeling betrayed and enraged, or scared and panicky? It's these kinds of specifics we want to start describing.

Right now, I want you to pull out your breakthrough journal.

In a moment, you're going to write down all the words that describe how you're feeling now about your breakup. When I do this exercise with clients, I often hear words like angry, hurt, betrayed, depressed, scared, overwhelmed, and so on.

Take a few minutes now to write down all these kinds of words that describe how *you* are feeling about your breakup.

Now that you have a collection of words describing your experience, I want you to look over that list and think about which ones feel most prominent and powerful for you right now; circle them.

Where You Are on Your Scale of Emotion?

The list of words that you just wrote is a big start to getting clear on where you are in your breakup. Now we're going to dive deeper and start to look at how intensely you're feeling particular emotions.

In a moment, I'm going to have you record how intensely you're feeling various emotions, on a scale of one to 10. This will help you get even clearer on your experience right now, but it's also going to be useful as a measurement of your progress as we move forward.

Maybe you'll gauge your sadness today at a nine out of 10. You're not going to instantly be at a one-level sadness tomorrow, but I am going to show you how to start dialing that nine down to an eight or a seven. Each day, you'll practice dialing down the emotions you don't want, and dialing up the emotions you do want—this is you putting to work the remote control to your mind.

These incremental steps will make a big difference. A level-nine sadness might mean you can't even get out of bed or make yourself a meal. A level-seven sadness might mean that you still feel pretty depressed, but you can get up, get dressed, and go to work. You still feel sad, sure, but that's already a huge improvement. Throughout these next weeks, you're going to learn how to cope better and more effectively to create lasting transformation.

In your breakthrough journal, take a moment to copy down the gauges below.

Anger

1   2   3   4   5   6   7   8   9   10

Sadness

1   2   3   4   5   6   7   8   9   10

Panic

1   2   3   4   5   6   7   8   9   10

Fear

1   2   3   4   5   6   7   8   9   10

Happiness

1   2   3   4   5   6   7   8   9   10

Optimism

1 2 3 4 5 6 7 8 9 10

Excitement

1 2 3 4 5 6 7 8 9 10

Also look back at the previous page, at the emotions you circled. If you circled any that aren't listed here, write those down also, with a scale of one to 10. Remember, everyone is different, and we want to create a benchmark of *your* unique experience.

In your breakthrough journal, record how intensely you're feeling them, on a scale between one (least intense) and 10 (most intense). Circle the appropriate number for each emotion.

You may have noticed that a few of the ones I've given you seemed a bit out of place. How could you possibly be feeling optimistic or excited about your breakup, right?

These measurements are also going to be how we look at your progress at the end of these 30 days. We'll take inventory of your emotions again at the end of this book, so that you can see how far you've come. However unlikely it might seem now, I know that you're going to see some jumps in happiness, optimism, and excitement.

Day 5

The Four Keys to
Surviving and Thriving

Today, we're looking at the four keys I've developed to surviving and thriving your split. These four key ideas will underpin everything we'll cover throughout these 30 days, and they'll be your guiding beacons as we move forward.

Key One: Take Responsibility

When you're in a relationship, it's natural for you to develop a codependency on and with your partner. The two of you make decisions together, create plans for your future together, handle the day-to-day aspects of life together, and so on. Some of us have a tendency to create a stronger codependency than others, but all of us do it to some degree; it's just part of being in a relationship.

When you break up, it can be difficult to let go of that codependency. Suddenly your partner is gone, and you're left feeling like part of your capacity to do this thing called life is gone too.

At the end of the day, though it may be hard to hear, the only one responsible for your life is *you*. This first key is all about taking responsibility for your life.

I had a client for whom this key was a particularly big factor.

This client was an older gentleman in his sixties. Before his split, he had been approaching his retirement. He and his wife had plans to travel the world when he retired, and he would constantly be talking about how excited he was for the trip of his lifetime, but soon after he retired, his wife left him, and all his plans for the future shattered.

He didn't go traveling. Instead, he just stayed home and complained to anyone who would listen about how his wife had ruined everything when she left, particularly how she ruined his trip of a lifetime.

He wasn't taking responsibility for his life or actions; he was still letting his ex be responsible for his life—and because she had left, his ability to move forward had left with her.

If we're constantly putting the blame and responsibility for our lives on someone else, it becomes difficult or impossible for us to move forward. This first key is all about shifting that and once again seeing ourselves as the sole author of our lives.

Key Two: Get Clarity

Clarity gives you power.

What do I mean by that?

Clarity is what gives you the ability to create and execute a plan for your future. Without clarity you can't have a plan, and without a plan it's almost impossible to move forward into the life that you want.

One of the most common fears I hear clients talk about is financial fear. Especially after a divorce, your financial future can be filled with uncertainty. I remember one client in particular who had always let her husband take care of the finances; he was the one who made money, handled money, and did everything else with money.

When this client found herself alone, she was in a panic. She had no idea what her current financial situation was like, let alone what her financial future would be. She had no clarity and no plan.

It was a scary step but an absolutely vital step for her to grit her teeth and start looking at her finances. She didn't even want to glance at a bank statement at first. I coached her along the way, building a clear understanding of her financial situation. It wasn't pleasant to do, but with that clarity she was able to develop a plan for her financial future, and with that clear plan, she was able to start taking action, and start creating a financial future she could be comfortable and happy in.

This holds true also for issues like what it is going to look like to be a single parent or co-parent, or how and when you're going to find a new place to live, or even just what it's going to look like for you to be single again. When you create clarity, you have the power to create the future you want. Even if you don't like what you see, you can create a plan to improve it. The simple act of creating clarity will dial down your overwhelm—there's nothing scarier than the unknown, and when you know your situation and have a plan to address it, it puts you back in the driver's seat.

Key Three: Take Back Your Control

Taking back your control is all about living through *your* choice, rather than living in reaction to your ex. As long as you're saying that you're feeling something or doing something because your ex did this or said that, your ex has all the power—because in your mind, you're giving them that power. It's like they're controlling you like a puppet on strings, even when they're not around.

Taking back your control is all about cutting those strings and climbing back in the driver's seat.

Remember that client whose post-retirement travel plans had been shattered? When he gave up his plans to travel the world because his ex had left, he had given her all the control. At one point in our sessions, I asked him a simple question: "Why don't you still go on the trip of your lifetime?"

He was shocked. He hadn't even considered that he could travel the world without his wife! But he decided to take back his control, and he made new plans for his trip—and here's the kicker—while he was traveling, he met someone, fell in love, and came back home in a new, thriving relationship. Talk about a happy ending!

Key Four: Focus on Moving Forward Positively

I had a client recently walk in my door sobbing hysterically. She was crying so hard she could barely speak, so I handed her a box of tissues and she kicked off her shoes and curled up on the couch.

It turned out that she had never been to the area where my clinic was, but she knew a friend who lived nearby, so she arranged to meet up with her friend before our session. The whole time that she was with her friend, she was telling the story of her breakup, in all its grisly detail.

For those hours with her friend, she was focusing entirely on the past.

When we focus on the past so intensely, it's nearly impossible for us to move forward. Imagine trying to drive to a destination but only staring in your rearview mirror; you're probably not going to get where you want to go, and you'll be lucky not to crash!

The same is true in your life.

The reason it's so upsetting to focus on the past is that you're quite literally reliving the experience. When it comes to emotions and feelings, the human brain can't really tell the difference between *imagining* a situation and actually *living* that situation. When you're repeating your sad breakup story for the hundredth time, you're putting yourself right back in the experience, bringing up all those feelings and hurt all over again, just as if it were literally happening again.

Luckily, however, this also holds true when we wrench ourselves around to focus on the future.

When you focus your mental energy on the future that you want to create, your brain puts you there, with all the emotions and feelings that bright future entails. When you focus on the future, you begin to actually *experience* that future—and next thing you know, you're living it.

How Well Are You Implementing These Keys Now?

Before we move forward, I want you to take stock of where you are now, with respect to these four keys for surviving and thriving.

Take out your breakthrough journal and write on a scale of one to 10 how well you're putting each key into practice. Also, write a few sentences for each about where you are or aren't putting that key into practice right now; maybe about how you're avoiding clarity about finances, or focusing your attention on the painful past, etc.

Just as in the previous chapter, this both helps you get clear on where you get to focus, and will also give us a gauge of your progress further on.

Day 6

What to Expect
When You Go Through a Split

As I've mentioned earlier, studies show that breaking up is often the second-most traumatic experience a person can go through—second only behind the death of a loved one.

It's not surprising, then, that the emotional journey of a split mirrors the emotional journey of grief.

You've probably heard of the five stages of grief. The idea first originated with psychiatrist Elisabeth Kübler-Ross in the 1960s. She was working with terminally ill patients and pinpointed five emotional stages that almost all patients and their loved ones would go through in the face of death.

After a split, you're facing a death of your own: the death of your relationship.

Just like someone grieving the physical death of a loved one, you too will face these five emotional stages, as you process through the end of your relationship.

The Loss Cycle

Before we look at each stage individually, it's important to note: the five stages are not a neat, linear order that everyone experiences the same way. In working through your split, I call these stages the loss cycle precisely because you don't experience and pass through them one at a time; instead, you'll probably find yourself cycling back and forth from one to another as you gradually move forward and through your loss.

With that in mind, let's look at each stage of the loss cycle.

Denial

Denial is the stage that most of us will encounter first.

In the denial stage, we simply refuse to believe or accept that the split—or the need for a split—is real. We'll rationalize away any problems, convince ourselves that things aren't as bad as they seem, and if a breakup *has* already taken place, we'll tell ourselves "It isn't *really* the end, we're just going through a tough spot."

When I first found that contact lens and eyelash in my personal drawer, I launched right into denial.

At first, I refused to believe that the evidence before my eyes could mean what I feared. Certainly, there wasn't infidelity in my marriage; I must be mistaken.

In the face of a cheating partner, denial is often the first response. We don't look because we don't want to see what's there. We assume we're just jealous and paranoid because it's too painful to consider reality.

Denial is a shock response; our bodies and minds literally go into a this-is-not-really-happening mode. If your partner left you, or if they sat you down for the breakup talk, you might remember your first response as being, "This can't really be happening."

Denial is a barrier to the emotional pain that's coming. It's your body's way of protecting you until you can deal with it.

Anger

In the anger stage, emotional energy rockets up.

The pain of the situation starts to bubble up, and anger is one of our first evolutionary responses to pain.

In the anger stage, our blood is boiling. How could this person, who I love and who I thought loved me, *do* this to me? How dare he or she?!

Our mind starts to race with fury, full of all the reasons this pain is *their* fault; how our ex has ruined everything. Anger is not a very introspective emotional state; all we can see is the blinding fury for everything that our ex has done or is doing wrong.

Anger is a stage that many people get stuck in—sometimes for months, or years, or even decades. Anger has a nasty tendency to self-perpetuate itself. We feel angry, so we lash out in some way—maybe through a bitter text, maybe through screaming in our ex's face, maybe through tossing his or her clothes and belongings out the window.

If we let it, anger can drive us to act in ways we'd have never thought ourselves capable of.

The problem is, when we act in these ways, we push our exes to respond in kind. We act out in anger towards them; they respond by acting in anger towards us, which only makes us *more* angry. The rage cycles and builds.

Anger in itself is not something to demonize or beat yourself up for. It's a natural part of the loss cycle; however, it can keep you stuck in a negative cycle. I remember one client of mine, Val. Val had split with her ex over a year prior, but had just let her anger fester on and on. She was still so angry when we started meeting that she'd taken to stalking her ex, parking outside the new home he shared with his girlfriend. She would sit there for hours on end, late into the night. She refused to sign the divorce papers, so the divorce was dragging on, costing her a fortune in legal fees. Her out-of-control anger was affecting her life, affecting her kids' lives, and she was just letting it spiral.

Anger is a natural part of the loss cycle, but not one to get stuck in. What's important is to know that it's coming, recognize it for what it is, and not get lost in an endless loop of anger. There are simple things you can do to dial down your anger and you will learn the techniques I shared with Val as we move through the chapters together.

Bargaining

Bargaining is the stage that often follows anger—as energy levels cool, we still haven't fully accepted the reality of the split, and we find ourselves willing to do *anything* to keep the relationship alive.

In the bargaining stage, the outward focus of anger starts to turn inward. You might notice thoughts like, "It's all my fault," or "Of course this is happening, because I _____."

We also start reasoning with ourselves here that we can save the relationship; that if we bend ourselves, twist ourselves, or change ourselves, we can salvage the relationship that we so desperately don't want to lose.

Maybe, if I just lose some weight, he'll find me attractive again and things will work. Or maybe, if I just start being more fun—go dancing, laugh more, smile more—she'll love me again. Or maybe, or maybe, or maybe…

If someone has ever broken up with you, that probably sounds familiar.

Bargaining is also a stage you'll go through if you're the one initiating a split, or if the breakup is mutual. You might find yourself reasoning that whatever it is you're dealing with *isn't* reason enough to break up. *Maybe*, you might tell yourself, *it shouldn't bother you so much that your partner is emotionally unavailable*—even though you know it does. Maybe his or her cheating on you *shouldn't* be a deal-breaker—even if, if you're being honest to your values, it is.

The bargaining stage brings along feelings of guilt and shame. As our blame turns inward, we'll often start beating ourselves up for all the ways we think we're not good enough or need to change.

This stage also brings with it a danger of sacrificing your integrity and inner truth. So often in this stage, we find ourselves

29

suddenly willing to betray our own values and self-worth—*anything* to salvage the relationship.

Depression

In the depression stage, energy levels are at their lowest.

Here, we're not trying to change anything anymore; we're not lashing out in anger, we're not bending ourselves to try to make things work.

In depression, all we see is despair.

This is when we find ourselves struggling to even get out of bed. We might be sleeping all the time or not at all. Apathy takes hold; it's impossible to do *anything*. *Because*, you might ask yourself, *what's the point?*

Depression is a stage filled with hopelessness. We don't expect the relationship we had to come back, and we don't see any hope for a new relationship in the future. It doesn't seem possible to ever be happy again, or to ever feel whole again. We feel broken.

With energy at its lowest, depression is the dark night of the loss cycle, the stage where it feels like the sun will never rise again; however, just like the darkest part of the night, it's also the stage that most often comes before the dawn.

Acceptance

In the acceptance stage, despite all the pain that came before, we find the sun does indeed rise again. Energy levels start to rise again, but where the high-energy rage of the anger stage points out towards our ex, the energy of acceptance fuels our own life.

In acceptance, pain starts to fade. That doesn't mean it disappears completely—that still often takes time—but that pain starts to decrease, and we begin moving forward.

In this stage, you'll find your thoughts focus more on the future. Hope and even excitement start to pop back into your life. Maybe you start thinking about dating again, and how much fun that will be, or maybe you start imagining what sort of adventures you can embark on now that you're single and calling all the shots.

Acceptance is the high-energy starting point that launches you into your bright new future.

Understanding Your Own Cycle and Where You Are

Remember, the loss cycle isn't a simple, linear progression; you might find yourself starting in the middle, or swinging back and forth between depression and bargaining for a while, or jumping between anger and denial.

Even the final stage—acceptance—isn't always a one-and-done finish line; you might well discover that you move back and forth through acceptance for a while before you finally move forward and out.

Everyone experiences each stage of the loss cycle differently, and everyone moves through that cycle differently. We also all progress through the cycle over different lengths of time. There's no right or wrong—just what's true for you.

What matters here is that you understand what to expect, recognize these stages in yourself, and are equipped to handle each.

In your breakthrough journal, write out a description of your own experience with each of these five different stages. If you've experienced a stage in your current breakup process, describe that. If you haven't yet been in a given stage with this particular journey, describe how you've experienced it in a past breakup.

*   *   *

Next, describe where you've struggled the most. Is anger the stage that hits you hardest, and you tend to spend the most time in? Or is that denial, bargaining, depression, or acceptance?

Whatever is true for you, describe where you tend to struggle the most and what that struggle looks like.

Finally, bring your attention to your current situation. In which stage of the loss cycle are you right now? Where are you among these five stages? In your breakthrough journal, record where you are right now and describe what that looks like for you.

Day 7

Building Your
Breakup Support Team

Your next step to creating a breakup plan that maximizes your breakthroughs is all about the people around you—your breakup support team.

When you're going through a split, how you process things is determined by more than just your own intentions and actions. It's also shaped by the people around you; the people you reach out to for solace, support, and guidance. Creating a breakup support team is about being intentional with who you reach out to; the people with which you surround yourself.

Now, let's be clear; there might well be people around you already who are part of your breakup process. Maybe you're already talking about things with your family, or a circle of friends—and that's great! But your breakup support team is about finding key individuals who will fill necessary roles; people who are there for you in very particular ways. Some of these people might already be in your life, but others you'll probably have to seek out.

For others of you, you might cringe at the thought of a breakup support team, precisely because right now you're isolating yourself in your breakup. I've worked with clients who, months after the split, had still not told a single person about his or her relationship ending; he or she had too much shame built up about it and were terrified at the thought of what people would think. If you're in this boat, I understand the fear, but to best process through your split, it's vital that you start bringing others on board.

Whatever your situation, this support team is going to be what lifts you up and acts as your foundation through this journey, so let's start building *your* support team, shall we?

Friends and Family

The first role to fill here is for friends and family. When it comes to your breakup support team, we're looking for one or two people from your friends and family whom you can count on to always have your long-term best interests in mind; people who can give you the advice and feedback you need to hear—with love and compassion.

And let's be honest—not every friend or family member fits that bill.

Imagine you just saw your ex post pictures on Facebook with his or her hot new partner, out partying and having a great time in a brand-new sports car. You're angry—really, really pissed. Right now, all you want to do is speed over to your ex's house, scratch up that brand-new car, and maybe toss a rock or two through a window.

You pick up your phone to reach out to a friend in this moment of crisis. Which of these two imaginary friends do you think belongs on your breakup support team? Friend A answers your call, listens to your story, and tells you that a keyed-up car is exactly what that scumbag deserves, and she'll be over to pick you up in 10 minutes; she'll even bring a pocketknife so you can slash those brand-new tires too. Friend B answers your call, listens to your story, and tells you that she completely understands why you would be upset. She then encourages you to take a few deep breaths and practice one of the exercises you learned from this book.

Which would you choose for your support team?

Exactly—Friend B, of course!

We probably all know some version of Friend A; someone who will enthusiastically jump on to whatever you're feeling and egg you on to something that might seem great in the moment, but doesn't exactly have your long-term interests in mind.

When it comes to your breakup support team, however, we're looking for someone like Friend B, who will listen compassionately but give you the support you *really* need for your long-term best interests. As tempting as it might be at times, keying up your ex's new car is never in your long-term interest.

Think over the loved ones in your life and decide which one or two people will best fill this role on your support team. In your breakthrough journal, write down the names of who you will reach out to.

Exercise Buddy

When you're going through emotional turmoil, it can sometimes be easy to lose sight of care for your physical body. Sometimes all you want to do all day is curl up in bed, grab a bag of chips, and stream Netflix until you pass out again.

Trust me, I get it; I've been there too, but pulling yourself out of bed and getting your body moving is going to make a huge impact on your mental and emotional states. Countless studies have shown the positive effects of exercise on mental and emotional health; you get your blood pumping, and those feel-good endorphins start to flow. Exercise is a great tool for alleviating your painful feelings and increasing the joyful feelings you want, both in the immediate moment, and over time with regular exercise, but again, sometimes exercise is the last thing on your mind.

That's where your exercise buddy comes in.

With your exercise buddy, you have someone who's going to keep you accountable to getting up and getting moving. It could be someone you'll go on walks or jogs with, someone you'll meet at the gym, or someone you'll play tennis with; whatever type of exercise suits you, your exercise buddy is right there with you.

An exercise buddy not only helps you keep up with your exercise, but also makes things more fun and keeps you motivated, and since you two will be an exercise team, you'll also be giving these same benefits to your exercise buddy—a true win-win.

Coach or Therapist

Connecting with a trained professional is going to exponentially increase your ability to process through your split and transform this crisis point into personal breakthroughs. Coaches and therapists are two distinct fields, both with their own strengths.

A coach will work with you in a future-oriented way, identifying goals and roadblocks, and supporting you in creating action plans to bust through those blocks to achieve your goals.

A therapist will work with you to look into your past to identify underlying issues that affect you, helping you to uncover and heal old wounds so that you're able to move forward.

There's no right or wrong answer when it comes to choosing to work with a coach or therapist. You probably have a gut sense of which would be most valuable for you, given your current situation and your own personal path. Some people choose to work with both a coach *and* a therapist, to tackle things from both sides, so to speak.

What matters here is that you find a trained professional to work with who will be with you on your journey. If you haven't yet ever worked with a coach or therapist, there's no time like the present; this is a vital role for your breakup support team and will prove invaluable in creating breakthroughs.

Financial Advisor

This role is not one that everyone will need on their own team. If your relationship at all entailed shared finances—joint accounts or one of you financially supporting the other—then you'll want a financial advisor. If your relationship did not at all entail shared finances, you can skip this one.

For those of you who *did* share finances in some way, a financial advisor is vital to moving forward. Whether you were simply sharing rent for a year or had joint finances through a 40-year marriage, your split means big changes in your financial life.

A financial advisor will work with you to create clarity on where you stand now and will help develop a plan for moving forward. The more intertwined your finances with your ex were, the more necessary it is for you to bring a trained financial professional onto your team.

Don't be anxious, as even if you don't like what you find you will be able to work with your financial advisor to put a plan in place to help you move forward.

Legal Advisor

Again, this role might not be one that you need to fill in processing your own split. If your breakup is a divorce, you absolutely need a legal advisor on your team. If you have any other legal connection to your ex—a shared lease or mortgage, children together, joint bank accounts, etc.—you'll want a legal advisor, whether you were married or not. A legal advisor is going to make sure you're on firm ground for the future, and that you're legally protected.

Whatever the tone of your breakup now, a legal advisor will make sure you know what you are legally entitled to, no matter what the future brings. Things might feel amicable and rosy now, so you might be tempted to think, "Oh, I don't need a lawyer; we can just figure things out between the two of us," but that's just setting yourself up for danger in the future. You never know when things might turn sour—and if that happens, the friendly agreements that seem good enough now might put you in legal jeopardy down the line.

You've probably heard the saying that an ounce of prevention is worth a pound of cure. Well, a lawyer today can prevent a legal nightmare tomorrow.

Assembling Your Team

At this point, you have, depending on your situation, three to five roles to fill for your breakup support team.

For the professionals you'll be working with, you want to be sure that you're bringing on someone that matches your own personal intentions and needs. Some lawyers, for example, are cut-throat bulldogs that will fight like fire; others have a more cooperative approach and will focus on building agreement and compromise between you and your ex. There's no right or wrong there, but you want to make sure you find the professional that suits your situation.

For your friends, family, and exercise buddy, you'll want to contact them and let them know you're bringing them onto your all-star team. With your exercise buddy, create a game-plan for how and when you'll work out together. Remember, clarity is key.

For your friends and family, let the one or two people you've chosen know that you see them as trusted sources of good advice, and that you'd like their support as you navigate your split.

In your breakthrough journal, you've already written down the names of the friends and family you'll bring onto your team. Also write down the names of a few people you might ask about being your exercise buddy. If you can't think of anyone, where could you look for one? People are often looking for work-out buddies; you might find them at your local gym, a yoga class, or networking sites, etc.

Also write in your breakthrough journal your plan to begin working with a coach or therapist. Are you working with one already? Do you know of any you could work with? Do you know of any friends or family who have worked with a coach or therapist who you think might be a good fit for you? If not, where will you start looking for one?

Finally, if they apply to you, write out the same plan for finding and beginning to work with a financial and/or legal advisor.

With your new team assembling around you, you're ready to kick your transformation into high gear.

Day 8

The Antidote to Negative Emotions

As you travel through the journey of your breakup, it's natural for you to experience a wide range of emotions.

Even in the most amicable split, there will be dark times of hurt and sorrow; painful breakups can bring negative emotions in waves that feel overwhelming.

Remember, there's no magic wand to making those negative emotions suddenly disappear, or jumping from a level-10 sadness to a level-10 joy. When you know how to use the remote control to your mind, you can dial your emotions up and down, bit by bit.

Over the next few days, you're going to learn and start practicing these tools to dial your emotions, but before we get into our first technique, a word of caution about some coping strategies you *won't* find in this book. These destructive patterns include:

- Throwing yourself into work, 24/7
- Drinking more than you normally would
- Drugs
- Over-eating
- Excessive partying

All these are popular ways to deal with negative emotions. The only problem?

They don't actually deal with the emotions at all; they only offer a temporary avoidance, and on top of that, they tend to only make the pain worse in the long run. They get in the way of genuine recovery, and things like lack of sleep, alcohol, and poor nutrition will heighten the severity of negative emotions.

What sets the tools you're going to learn here apart from those self-destructive patterns is that we aren't going to avoid the emotions; we're going to face them head on and transform them.

Some of these tools might feel uncomfortable at times, but this head-on approach is what will assuage your negative emotions in a sustainable way, allowing you to truly take back control of your emotions and move forward.

Think of those negative emotions like a roller coaster that you're strapped into—and terrified of. You're climbing that first huge hill—heart racing, wishing you could just magically be back on solid ground; you'd give anything to take back this awful decision and just teleport away. But then you crest the hill, fly through the coaster, and coast back to the station laughing your head off.

The next time you get on a roller coaster, you might still get butterflies in your stomach at the start, but each time it gets a little easier, until you find yourself enjoying the whole process.

It's the exact same pattern here.

When you start using these tools to face your negative emotions, you'll find the process isn't quite as awful as you expect, and you'll experience the relief of dialing down those negative emotions. Then every time you practice it, it becomes just a little bit easier, until you find yourself dialing down and dialing up with ease. That's the goal here, and that's what is going to create breakthroughs and transformation in every area of your life.

Let's turn now to our first technique, the antidote to negative emotions: *Gratitude*.

Gratitude is one of the most powerful mindsets human beings can step into. When we begin to focus on gratitude, the intensity of negative emotions cools down.

In a moment, you're going to pull out your breakthrough journal and simply start writing as much as you can think of that you're grateful for.

When you're deep into a negative emotional experience, this can feel difficult at first, and that's ok. The things you list can either be big or small. Maybe you're grateful for your best friend, who you know will be there for you. Maybe you're grateful for the really cozy pair of socks that you're wearing. The point here is to shift your focus towards gratitude, inch by inch.

Keep adding to your list for at least a few minutes, until you've got a solid collection written down and can't think of any more. Write your gratitude list now.

Once you've completed this exercise, reflect on the experience: how have you noticed a decreased shift in your negative emotions? At what level were those emotions before the exercise and what are they now?

You'll want to keep this list with you. When you start to feel those negative emotions building up, pull out your gratitude list and read through it, focusing on each item and your feelings about them. Doing so will turn the dial on those painful emotions, de-intensifying them. You can also repeat this exercise and write a new gratitude list, to the same effect.

This attitude of gratitude is an antidote that you can pull out at any time—and the more you do, the more effective and effortless the technique becomes.

Day 9

Letting Go of Your Baggage

Today, you're going to start dropping your baggage.

When I talk about baggage, I'm talking about the negativity that holds you back and weighs you down. In part, this includes the negative emotions we've looked at throughout the past week and a half, but baggage is about more than just those negative emotions—it includes:

- Negative emotions
- Negative thoughts—the self-defeating thoughts that run through your head throughout the day, like "I'm just never good enough," or "I'm ugly," or "I'm never going to find love again."
- Worries
- Bad experiences from your past
- Problems you're facing
- Negative words and phrases
- Fears
- Stresses

We shove all these painful, anxiety-causing, grief-inducing thoughts and feelings into luggage and drag them around with us as baggage. Just reading that list, you are probably already thinking about some of your own personal baggage.

43

Wouldn't it be wonderful and liberating to simply let go of all that baggage? Well that's what we're going to start doing today.

This exercise might push your comfort zone. You might feel uncomfortable with it the first time, and that's ok, but remember, you committed to playing full out, so dive in with me. I promise the joy of feeling your baggage drop away is worth it.

For this technique, I want you to first look back at the above list of what gets packed into our baggage—the negative emotions, thoughts, worries, and so on. As you look over the list, start to bring to mind your own baggage. What negative emotions, thoughts, and worries fill your head and heart during the day? What bad experiences from your past still haunt you? What fears, problems, and stresses are you dealing with? I know it's uncomfortable, but it's part of the process.

Turn your attention to your body and how you feel right now. We all carry our baggage differently. For some of us, it's a feeling of heavy tightness in our chest. For others, it feels like a weight pushing down on our shoulders, or sinking down in our stomach. For some, it feels like dragging behind us a train of bags tied to our waist. What does your baggage look like? How does it feel?

Turn to a blank page in your breakthrough journal and draw where your baggage is. You don't have to be an artist; it can be as simple as a stick figure with a big blob pushing down on its shoulders. As best you can, put down on the page the placement, the feel, and the shape of your baggage.

All around this picture, I want you to add in what you've packed into your baggage. Again, looking at the list above of what's in our baggage, fill the paper with all you can think of; the negative emotions that affect you most, negative thoughts you have, worries, and so on. You can write these down in words, or draw them in pictures, add color; whatever works for you.

With this stark illustration of your baggage, now we're going to get clear on how that baggage affects your life. Turning to a new page in your breakthrough journal, write out answers to each of the following questions:

1. How does your baggage make you feel?
2. How does your baggage affect your life?
3. What will your life be like in 1 year if you continue to hold onto it?
4. What will your life be like in 5 years if you continue to hold onto it?
5. What will your life be like in 10 years if you continue to hold onto it?

I know it's not easy going through this, and it can bring up a lot of negativity to think about, but this is all part of the journey. You're doing some real transformative work here, and you should be proud of yourself for playing all out and diving in.

We're now going to shift our focus towards positivity, so first shake yourself off a bit; maybe take a quick walk around the room.

I want you to imagine now being free of all your baggage. Imagine what it would be like to simply drop all your baggage and wipe your slate completely clean.

With that vision in mind, write out answers to these three questions, starting on a new page in your breakthrough journal:

1. How will you feel when you've dropped all your baggage?
2. How will your life be improved?
3. What positive emotions will replace the negative emotions?

Now we're going to start practicing how exactly to let go of these negative emotions and drop your baggage—and I know this is the part you've probably been looking forward to. This is another part that might be challenging for you. I'm going to have you push your comfort zone and face these emotions head-on, but I'm right here with you.

First, I want you to turn back again to the picture you drew of your baggage; focus on that swarm of negativity. I want you to pick out the three negative emotions that are most impacting you right now; the ones that hit you hardest. Maybe anger, depression, shame, or fear—whatever the most powerful negative emotions are for you.

Put a bookmark or folded corner on the page with the gratitude list you created yesterday. You're going to have this gratitude list ready to go as we practice transforming negative emotions into positive ones of gratitude and happiness. Remember, gratitude is your antidote.

I'm going to describe the rest of the exercise, and I want you to read through it all, then put this book down and do it. When you do, make sure there won't be any distractions, so turn your phone off, close your door, shut your computer down; anything that ensures you can be fully immersed in your experience.

What you're going to do is first draw three circles in your breakthrough journal, just like the image on the next page.

Write the three most powerful negative emotions you identified earlier in the three empty circles you've drawn. I want you to imagine yourself standing on top of that top circle, and jumping down into that first negative emotion, as if you were jumping into a big pool of it.

You're going to imagine what it looks like, feels like, sounds like to be *fully immersed* in this emotion; what it feels like and where you feel it.

This isn't the time to hold back, so really go deep into it. If you feel uncomfortable with this, you're doing it right. I *want* you to feel uncomfortable here because if you don't push your comfort zone, you're not going to grow. Push yourself here and really let this negative emotion wash over you.

After 20 or 30 seconds of your first emotion, you're going to drop down and dive into your second emotion and do the same thing. What does it feel like to be immersed in this? What are the sensations, sounds, sights?

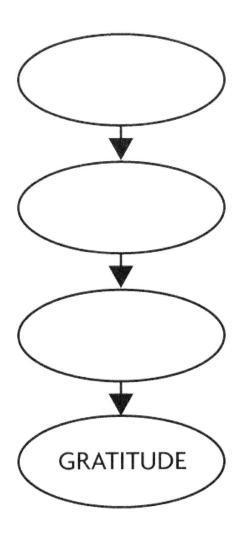

After 20 or 30 seconds here, drop down to your third emotion and immerse yourself in the experience here.

I know it's uncomfortable, but push through. It's ok if you cry.

After 20 or 30 seconds in your third emotion, turn to your gratitude list. Start reading through each item on your list and focus on all of the things in your life that have you feeling like a million bucks. Keep reading through your gratitude list and centering yourself in each item you're grateful for until you start to feel better.

Now, you get to put that exercise into action. It might be tough, but I know you can do it. I'll see you on the other side.

*   *   *

Good work! I know that wasn't easy, but now you're really starting to shift your mental and emotional patterns. This is the breakthrough work here.

Grab the picture you drew of your baggage. This is going to get uncomfortable again, but I want you to focus on the baggage. Hold the picture in front of you and dive into it; let it fill you up until you're just absolutely sick of it and you just can't take it anymore, until you can't stand even *one* more second of it.

And then tear it out of your journal and *rip it up*!

Tear that sheet up into tiny little pieces, and throw those pieces as far away as you can.

As you throw those scraps away, imagine that you're throwing your baggage with it; all those negative emotions and thoughts just flying away from you, once and for all!

When you're in this clean space, having thrown all that baggage away, open your breakthrough journal again and write responses to these three questions:

1. What are you going to do differently now?
2. What can you do now that you couldn't do before?
3. How has your life changed?

Remember, we're not looking for a magic-wand instant solution here; this is all about dialing down. We bring up those negative emotions, dial them down, then throw all the baggage away from us.

Each time you practice this, the baggage you drop shrinks a bit smaller—a bit lighter. Step by step, you drop that baggage for good, bringing down its intensity lower and lower.

Before you know it, you're walking with a spring in your step and the weight of all that negativity is replaced with the positive emotions you want in your life.

That's the fantastic life you deserve, and you're already creating it.

Day 10
Flip-It

During your breakup journey, there are going to be bright moments and dark moments; yes, even in the most breakthrough-oriented split, there will be dark moments. There's no magic wand to ensure that you'll never have another dark, painful moment again, but remember, our mission here is to give you the remote control to your mind so you can minimize and assuage those dark points; it's not an on-and-off light switch, but a dimmer switch.

Wouldn't it be great to have a tool like a mental dimmer switch that gives you the power to start bringing some lights to your darkest moments? Luckily, that's exactly what this next tool does.

Flip-it is one of the simplest tools I'm going to give you, but also one of the most powerful. It's easy to practice and will boost your spirits when you most need it. This is a technique I created to help me through the darkest days of my own breakup.

Flip-It

When you're in a dark moment, first identify what the situation precisely is that is weighing you down. Maybe it's late evening and you find yourself eating dinner alone. Perhaps you're thinking about the vacation ideas you and your ex had, and now you're lamenting that you have no one to go on adventures with.

Maybe you and your ex have children together and you've just dropped the kids off for their weekend away from you.

Next, look for the good in that situation.

That's essentially it!

Now, you might be rolling your eyes and saying, "Sara, that sounds lovely, but there's *nothing* good about this. Period."

Ok, I hear you. I've felt that way too and have worked with hundreds of clients who have described their situation in exactly the same way, but if you look for it, there is always something good.

A few years ago, I was working with one woman named Beth. Beth had just recently finalized a painful divorce with her ex, Jeremy. Beth and Jeremy had two young children together, and as part of their divorce agreement, the kids would spend two full weekends a month with Jeremy.

Beth was agonized when Jeremy would come to pick the kids up. When they left, she would close the door behind them, and literally collapse onto the floor in tears. She'd spend the rest of the weekend crying, thinking constantly about her kids, feeling awful and alone, and counting down the minutes until she could go pick them up.

When I introduced flip-it to her and encouraged to practice it with those moments, Beth was downright indignant. "Sara," she said, "I love these kids more than anything in the world. They're my light and joy. What could *possibly* be good about having them torn away from me twice a month?"

I encouraged her to push forward with it; yes, it's painful; yes, there are tons of very true reasons why this is so awful, but if there was *something* good about it, what might it be?

Beth thought for a few minutes.

"Well," she eventually started, "with the kids gone, I *do* have a lot of time for myself. That could be something good; usually, all my time goes to work or the kids."

"Ok," I encouraged her, "and with that time for yourself, what could be good there?"

She visibly perked up, just a little bit. "You know, I've always wanted to start a business making and selling jewelry. I used to make jewelry, just for friends and family, and I was pretty good at it, but with kids, I don't have time for it anymore. Maybe I could start doing that again?"

Bingo. I encouraged her to focus on that and to practice the flip-it technique each time Jeremy picked up the kids for a weekend.

Fast forward a few months: Beth is making jewelry again, and has started selling her work on online. She's making extra income, and has revitalized a hobby she loves. Now, when the kids leave for their weekend with her ex, sure, she's still sad about it; she still misses them when they're gone, but she's also excited to run to her workroom and start making jewelry, living a dream she'd almost written off and forgotten.

Flip-it isn't about denying the darkness or making yourself wrong for how you feel about any situation. Did Beth have good reasons to feel such sorrow and agony when her children left for a weekend? Of course!

Flip-it is about *finding the good* in a situation and redirecting your focus there. Even when it might *seem* impossible—like the saying goes, every cloud has a silver lining.

In your breakthrough journal now, I want you to practice flipping it. Think of a specific situation that is causing you pain in your breakup, then for one minute, focus on looking for the good in that situation. What positives does this bring? What possible benefits could it have for you?

Write down whatever positives you can think of. If you come up with some in a minute, great; if it takes you longer the first time, that's ok; push through until you come up with at least one.

*　　*　　*

Flip-it is a strategy that gets easier each time. You can practice it anywhere—don't worry if you're not able to write things down—and it only needs to take a minute. And remember, the breakthroughs you're creating here will spread throughout your life. This is a technique you can practice in any area of your life. Problem at work? Flip it. Haven't yet lost the weight you want? Flip it. Argument with your mother? Flip it.

The more you practice it, the more flip-it will start to become second nature. You'll find that before long, you start automatically seeing the good in any painful situation. As soon as the clouds start rolling in, you'll find yourself smiling at those bright, silver linings.

Day 11

Coping Strategies—Heartbreak

Over the next few days, we're going to dive into coping strategies to use for specific aspects of the aftermath of a breakup. Today, we focus on heartbreak.

Heartbreak is a feeling that can be difficult to describe, but when you're in it, you know it, and if you've picked up this book, odds are you know all too well what we're talking about here.

It's that state of mind in which suddenly all the sad songs on the radio make sense like they never did before. It seems like every station is playing Adele, and suddenly you *get it*.

Heartbreak can bring a physical pain, like you've been punched in the chest—like your heart is literally aching, shattered, screaming in pain. It can feel as though you've had part of yourself ripped away, leaving behind a hollow emptiness in your chest or stomach.

What exactly heartbreak feels like and what images ring most true differs from person to person, but all of us have been there; it's part of being human. Maybe this is your first time being plunged into these cold waters of life; maybe you've been here before and are even more distressed because you thought that your last relationship would be the one to never send you here.

Whatever your own situation, remember—you are not alone.

Where you are right now—I've been there too, and so has everyone you love and respect. It sucks, but it's a part of life that we all face sooner or later.

Luckily, there are some great strategies I've gathered and developed over the years to decrease the pain you're feeling. Below is a list of these coping strategies. There is a lot here, but don't be overwhelmed; you don't need to start practicing each one right now. There are a few strategies I'll invite you to use to do some immediate work in your breakthrough journal, but many of these are strategies you can use simply whenever you feel the need throughout this process.

As you read through these strategies, make a note in your breakthrough journal of at least three or four that particularly resonate with you, and which you'll start to put into practice today.

Coping Strategies—Heartbreak

When you feel overwhelmed, take some slow, deep breaths.

This first strategy is one of the simplest, but you will be amazed at how effective it can be.

Our states of mind and emotions are intimately tied to our physiology and physical body. When you're deep in the pain of heartbreak and feeling overwhelmed, your body and physiology starts to change, whether you realize it or not. We start to take short, shallow breaths, and our hearts begin to race.

One effect of that shallow breathing is that you start bringing less oxygen into your body and stress hormones begin to release. This exacerbates the overwhelm and heartbreak you're feeling, and everything escalates in a feedback loop. Taking slow, deep breaths interrupts and reverses this destructive cycle.

When you breathe deeply, your muscles and brain receive an influx of the oxygen they were craving. You stop the release of stress hormones and your body will start to release feel-good neurotransmitters like serotonin and dopamine. The simplified version: deep breathing literally forces your body into calming and feeling good.

The first time you practice this, you'll be amazed at how powerful this simple physical shift can be.

Take off the rose-tinted glasses and focus on the things that were not perfect in your relationship.

When we're fresh into a breakup, it's natural to look back longingly at all the great things from your relationship. You'll remember all the good times—and probably remember them even better than they were at the time—and that wave of memories makes your feelings of loss and emptiness even stronger. It's time you take off the rose-tinted glasses you've duct-taped to your face.

No relationship is perfect and if you've broken up—whether it was an amicable split or a vicious one, whether you initiated the split or your ex did—I can guarantee there was a lot in your past relationship that wasn't all that great. When we keep those rose-tinted glasses on, though, we don't see all that.

It's time to get realistic about the things you didn't like about your relationship. This realism and clear-eyed view of things will soothe your heartbreak now and also set the stage for creating a great new relationship in the future; one that works and lasts.

Before we begin that exercise, though, it's important to also keep in mind that we don't want to swing too far to the *other* side of the spectrum. You don't need to or want to demonize everything from your past relationship. Realism is about seeing what worked and what was great alongside what didn't work and what you didn't like.

When I was married, I would tell you that my wedding day was one of the most magical, joyful days of my life. Now that I'm divorced, guess what—it is still one of the most special and happy days of my life! I can still treasure that memory and honor it for what it was while also being realistic about everything that didn't work.

Maybe you remember fondly how you and your ex used to walk down to the river and talk each weekend. Lovely! But what you might not be thinking about now is how every time you did, he'd just talk about work the whole time and you never felt he was listening to you.

This exercise is about creating that realistic view of your past relationship. When you take off the rose-tinted glasses, healing becomes easier.

In your breakthrough journal now, I want you to list everything that you can think of that you were *not* happy with in your relationship.

Stop telling your story because this causes you to re-experience the negative emotions.

Remember Holly, the woman we discussed earlier who was shocked to realize just how much she was talking about her ex? It's completely natural to want to keep telling the story of your breakup, but it doesn't help you in the long run.

When you've gone through a split, you've lost the intimacy and connection that the partnership brought you, so it's natural for you to seek emotional connection with others. This is what can make retelling your story so tempting—when you tell your sad story, you get the solace and comfort and emotional care that you're craving—but, when you retell the story, you relive it. We all know someone who does nothing but moan about their ex to anyone who will listen; you don't want to be that person.

It's time to start telling new stories, refocusing your attention and your connection with the people around you. If you feel like you're overwhelmed by the split and have nothing else to talk about, that's ok too; all you have to do is get out there and start creating new stories.

Use your ex's initial, not his or her name.

Your ex's name right now is tied to a whole boatload of emotional turmoil and pain, so stop using his or her name; it might sound silly, but it works. Instead of using his or her name, start using the first initial. Was your ex named Richard? Great, now he's r. Brianna? Now she's b. You'll notice, I'm not even using capital letters. They don't deserve capital letters. Just give them nice, little, lowercase initials. That's it. When you rename your ex in this way, you minimize the emotional weight he or she has for you.

Some clients I work with have already done some renaming of their own. They've renamed their ex's contact info in their phone as something like, "Asshole" or "Cheating Bastard." While that might feel good in the moment, you're not actually decreasing the emotional weight that his or her name has; you're only highlighting the *negative* emotional weight.

Go into your phone now and rename your ex's contact, not to an insult, but just to that tiny little lowercase initial—so small that it couldn't possible carry much emotional weight. And when you talk about him or her, do the same.

Surround yourself with people that make you feel good about yourself and can help you move forward.

If you want to feel good, surround yourself with people who make you feel good. It's simple and obvious, but it's also shocking how many people don't do this.

There are people in your life who will feed the negativity you're feeling right now. They might not mean to, but they'll just keep you stuck where you are by wanting to talk about all the nasty, little details of your split, or maybe they make snide remarks about you that only feed the negative self-talk in your head.

Then there are people who help push you forward and build you up, who help you focus on the things you enjoy in life, and who are there to compliment you when you're feeling down. These are the people you want to surround yourself with.

Your breakup support team is your foundation here, but don't limit it just to them. The friends and communities that build you up and make you feel good—seek them out; spend your time there; let their love and support carry you forward.

Plan your days so that you keep busy, get out of the house, and keep active.

It can be tempting to just stay at home all day with the lights off, lying in bed, and wallowing in your heartbreak, but don't! When you get out in the world and get busy, you turn your attention to new things and you start creating new stories and great, new memories. It might feel like a slog at first, but the more you do it, the easier it gets—and the more you'll dial down your heartbreak.

Know that it's ok to cry and that crying can be an important part of your healing process.

Crying is ok. It can be healing and can bring about a release of tension and stress. You might have a voice in your head telling you, "Big girls don't cry," or "Boys don't cry." Ignore that voice.

If you feel the urge to cry, know that it's ok, and it might just be the healing catharsis you need.

Write a diary about how you are feeling, as this is cathartic and a good way to free up your head space.

If you feel overwhelmed with heartbreak, there's a simple trick to getting it out of your head and freeing space to move forward: just write it out.

When you put your thoughts and feelings on paper, you experience the catharsis of facing them head on and letting them out. You'll find that as soon as you write down the experience, the volume of it in your head turns down; it's almost as if you've literally transferred the feelings and thoughts out of your head and down onto the page—and once they're written out, you're able to move forward.

You can use your breakthrough journal to write out your feelings and thoughts when they're overwhelming, or you could start a dedicated diary to write in every day.

Day 12

Coping Strategies—Betrayal

Betrayal is one of the most painful and challenging experiences to overcome.

When we think about betrayal in terms of relationships and breakups, we tend to focus on infidelity—one partner going out and cheating. Many of you reading this have likely experienced that sort of betrayal in your split; maybe you found out your ex was carrying on an affair behind your back, or he or she had hooked up with someone at a bar.

Infidelity and the feelings of betrayal can extend beyond just want happened during the official timeline of your relationship. Perhaps your ex went out and started dating someone new just days after your breakup; in a case like that, you're likely to be feeling betrayed as well. Betrayal can extend even beyond that kind of infidelity too.

Betrayal is about a breach of your trust, your boundaries, or your values. When someone cheats on you, or when he or she starts dating someone new immediately after splitting from you, that's almost certainly going to be a breach of your trust, boundaries, and values, but even if your situation isn't reflected in any of that sort of betrayal, odds are the relationship you're healing from *did* bring a sense of betrayal in some way.

Maybe you trusted him when he said he'd love you forever—and then he broke that promise when he left. Maybe you thought that you'd finally met someone who would treat you well, but then you were betrayed when she started putting you down and treating you poorly. You might even be feeling betrayed but you're not sure why, and that's ok too; sometimes we're not aware of our own boundaries and values until we really look closely.

Whatever your own situation, a sense of betrayal is probably part of your breakup journey. Today, we're going to focus our attention on how to cope with that feeling.

Jumping Out of the Hamster Wheel

One of the most common and most natural responses to feeling betrayed is to start asking yourself what I call hamster-wheel questions. These are the questions we tend to start obsessing over as we try to make sense of what happened. These questions include:

- *Why did he or she do it?*
- *What is wrong with me?*
- *Why aren't I enough?*
- *Who else knows about it?*
- *What did I do to deserve this?*
- *What else has he or she been dishonest about?*

Why do I call them hamster-wheel questions? Because no matter how long you spend on them, how much you think about them, or how badly you want to figure them out, you're never going to get anywhere. Just like a hamster in a wheel, your mind will run itself exhausted, but you'll still be right where you started.

I'm going to share with you a secret about your brain—if you ask it a question, it *will* do everything it can to find an answer. We're going to dig deeper into this truth, and learn how to use it for your benefit in a couple weeks, but for now, it's important to understand that those hamster-wheel questions only dig you deeper into the hole.

If you ask yourself "Why aren't I enough?" or "What did I do to deserve this?" you're not going to create any closure or clarity for yourself, but your brain will do everything it can to find answers to those questions, until you're so overwhelmed with self-criticism you can hardly move.

So, just jump out of the hamster wheel.

Understand that it's natural for those self-doubting questions to pop up, but the best thing you can do is just turn your attention elsewhere. We will cover in more detail how to do this later on.

Stop the Social Media Self-Harming

This is one of the easiest traps to fall into, and so one of the most important strategies for you to take on is to quit the cyberstalking!

These days, we are all connected through some forms of social media. Odds are you have a Facebook, Twitter, Instagram, or Snapchat account; or whatever new platform has become popular in the last month. And if you've recently gone through a split, odds are you're still connected with your ex on any platform you are both on.

You know the temptation here—you jump on Facebook or Instagram to see what your ex is up to and find yourself spending hours scrolling through their pictures and posts, and, oh boy, does it hurt.

I call this social media self-harming. Watching what your ex is up to without you, while you're still processing a split, is only ever going to cause you fresh heartache and pain.

A few years back, I was working with a woman named Chelsea whose ex had left her for a new, younger girlfriend. Chelsea would see them on Facebook posting pictures dancing at clubs, going on trips, out for dinner. Every picture cut Chelsea straight to the heart. Her ex used to complain that Chelsea wasn't fun or interesting enough, and now she was seeing her replacement online—and the new girlfriend seemed to have all the young, fun, interesting qualities that Chelsea had been criticized for lacking.

Every time Chelsea would go on a cyberstalking tour, she'd end up in tears, feeling even worse about herself.

I helped Chelsea see that this was a cycle she needed to eject from, so she unfriended and unfollowed her ex on social media—and found that it allowed her to refocus her attention and start to move on.

Months later, Chelsea ran into the new girlfriend at a grocery store. At that point, Chelsea had moved forward with her own life, and so meeting the new girlfriend in person didn't hurt. Out of curiosity, Chelsea struck up a conversation, and guess what? Chelsea discovered that her replacement wasn't nearly the perfect dream girl that she'd built up in her head. The woman only seemed to able to talk about clubbing and partying. She wasn't all that interesting, and without the Instagram filters and perfectly-angled Facebook selfies, she wasn't even as pretty as she looked online.

A few weeks later, Chelsea's ex was begging her to take him back; he was talking about missing how interesting and fun Chelsea was, and how the woman he left Chelsea for was dull and one-dimensional. Chelsea decided that she was better off without her ex—and there's a valuable lesson here.

We all tend to curate a very particular image online. If your ex has a new boyfriend or girlfriend, he or she is probably going to post only the most glamorous snapshots and selfies they can manage. All of that is only going to hurt you, and it's going to feed the self-defeating stories you have about not being good enough, but more often than not, the picture we get from social media is far from the full truth.

Stop comparing your behind-the-scenes to your ex's staged highlight reel, and stop the social media self-harming.

Evaluating and Re-Establishing Your Boundaries

When we're in a relationship, we tend to make compromises. That's a necessary part of the game, and when done mindfully, it's a healthy part of relationships.

Maybe you love Indian takeout—if it were up to you, anytime you didn't feel like cooking dinner and just wanted a quick meal, you'd be calling up the Indian restaurant down the street—but perhaps your partner isn't wild about Indian food, and prefers Thai. In a relationship, maybe the two of you agree to alternate between the two—Indian food one week you order in and Thai food the next. That's perfectly reasonable; maybe you'll even discover a new type of food you'll love!

Although compromising is important, personal boundaries are also vitally important. Your personal boundaries define what is acceptable behavior in a relationship and what is not. Your boundaries are *yours*, and no one else can tell you what they should be. For some of us, casual flirting might be fine, as long as it doesn't turn into anything physical or seriously emotional. For others, that sort of flirting already crosses a boundary. There's no right answer, only what is true for *you*.

In relationships, sometimes boundaries start to slip. We want to make our partner happy and we want to make the relationship work, so we can be tempted to ignore our own boundaries. When we compromise our boundaries, however, we're not just being flexible or accommodating with our partner—we're sacrificing our values, and when we sacrifice our values, we lose an important part of who we are.

Remember last week when we focused on the loss cycle? This boundary-sacrificing pitfall becomes particularly dangerous when we're in the bargaining stage of the loss cycle, but oftentimes it was already at play in the relationship before the split.

As you move forward, it's important for you to evaluate and re-establish your own personal boundaries. As you cope with betrayal, you have an opportunity to become conscious of where you may have been sacrificing your boundaries and values.

For this exercise, turn to a blank page in your breakthrough journal. First, spend at least a few minutes writing out the areas or ways you feel betrayed by your ex, either during your relationship or through the split.

Next, spend some time identifying the boundaries that were crossed. If you're feeling betrayed, one or more of your boundaries was crossed, and it's important to bring clarity to this. Some are clear and simple—maybe you feel betrayed by your ex cheating, which crossed the boundary of sexual fidelity. Others are more subtle—maybe you felt betrayed when your ex would go a day or two without responding to your calls, which crossed a boundary of yours about communication.

Remember, there is no right list when it comes to personal boundaries; boundaries are your own—no one else's. Now, spend five minutes evaluating where you get to strengthen your boundaries or your commitment to them. You might see where some boundaries were crossed and you were quick to respond; maybe you found out your ex was cheating and you ended the relationship right there.

You might also see some boundaries that you bent or ignored and started sacrificing your own values. Maybe your ex would become verbally and emotionally cruel when he or she drank, but you let it slide or ignored it. Maybe she started guilting you about spending time with your friends, so you sacrificed something important to you for the sake of keeping her happy.

Make a list of the boundaries you're identifying, and highlight the ones that you think you could improve your commitment to in relationships. This is going to be vital insight for you when we turn our attention to dating again and clarifying your ideal relationship.

One client I worked with, Gina, discovered in our time together just how much she'd sacrificed her boundaries in her relationship. Gina's ex-husband, Simon, would constantly criticize her appearance. He told her he didn't like when she wore her hair up, so Gina started wearing it down all the time. He would tell her that she looked like a man from certain angles, and Gina quickly started feeling overwhelmingly self-conscious about her looks, convinced that she was unattractive.

Simon didn't like spending time with Gina's family, so Gina started visiting them less and less, making excuses about being too busy. He didn't like her spending time with friends either, so she started cutting back there too. Her social life dwindled until her friends stopped even inviting her out.

At the time, Gina thought she was just showing her husband how much she loved him, but she didn't realize there were unhealthy dynamics going on. Looking back in our coaching sessions, she discovered just how much she had sacrificed and how many of her boundaries she'd crossed. She realized that she had a lot of boundaries to rebuild before starting a new relationship.

Making Small Changes Now

When dealing with betrayal and crossed boundaries, it's important for you to begin re-establishing your own sense of autonomy—that your life is *yours*, and that you get to create it however you want.

One of the most forwarding coping strategies is a simple one. Start making small changes to your life that strengthen your sense of self, which is going to start rebuilding your confidence and increasing your happiness.

Think about some of the compromises you made in your relationship—whether healthy ones or unhealthy ones. Now that you're not in that relationship, you get to focus all your attention on you.

Maybe you've gotten used to splitting your takeout orders between Indian and Thai food, but now you get to just stick with that Indian food you love. Maybe the furniture in your bedroom isn't arranged quite how you would choose, but the two of you compromised on it, so you get to change it to how you want it. Maybe you wanted bright orange curtains, but your ex wasn't into it, so the two of you chose beige—well, now you get to go full-neon orange!

Wear a new color, get a makeover, visit a different supermarket, drive a new way to work; if you do what you've always done, you will get the same results, and you'll stay in the same mindset.

Any small changes like these might not seem like a big deal, but redesigning your life as you want it is going to propel you forward into the passionate, fulfilled future you want.

In your breakthrough journal, write a list of small things that you can do—starting right now—to reflect what you want your life to look like. Choose at least one of these to put into action today.

Day 13

Coping Strategies—
Dealing with Your Ex

Part of the difficulty in moving on from a split is the reality that, although your ex is no longer in a relationship with you, he or she hasn't disappeared from the face of the planet. This means that, for better or worse, you'll need to be prepared to cope with him due to no longer being in a relationship with him. Parts of today's chapter won't apply to everyone, since every situation is unique.

The first section, which takes a look at coping strategies to handle possibly seeing your ex again, *is* something that will apply to just about everyone. Odds are, even though you and your ex have split, you still live in the same general area; there's a good chance that the two of you have grown accustomed to the same shops, hangout spots, and places to have fun, so there's a chance you'll run into him or her from time to time. Even if you were in a long-distance relationship, or you or your ex have moved away, the two of you still probably have mutual friends or acquaintances, so you'll want to have strategies ready to cope with possibly seeing him or her again.

The second section takes a look at considering whether you were in an unhealthy or abusive relationship, and suggests some coping strategies to deal with such a situation. It's an unfortunate truth that abusive relationships are a reality for far too many people in the world.

The third section focuses on coping strategies for when you and your ex have children together. In a case like this, you and your ex are probably going to be in contact far more often than you otherwise would, so I provide you with tools and strategies to make the new arrangement work—and work best for you.

Seeing Your Ex Again—Mind Movies

Even if you live in a large city, or not very close to your ex, there's always a chance of running into him or her again. Sometimes, even just the *thought* of seeing him or her can bring along overwhelming anxiety. I've worked with clients who would do everything possible to avoid going to a grocery store, out of fear of seeing their exes in the aisles.

The tool I'm going to introduce you to today will help ease any fears or anxiety, and also set you up for success if and when you *do* encounter your ex. Mind movies is a technique I learned from my friend, Paul McKenna, a behavioral scientist and expert in neuro-linguistic programming and motivation.

Creating a mind movie is all about running through a scenario in your imagination, in a way that has you handle a difficult situation well. This gives you the mental practice and confidence both to know you *can* handle it, and to have practiced the encounter before it ever occurs. Remember, your brain doesn't really know the difference between real and imaginary, so when you practice scenarios in your head with mind movies, it will feel like second nature if you ever have to put them to work in the real world.

To create a mind movie, first you'll pick a particular scenario that you're worried about. Maybe it's something sort of general, like running into your ex at the grocery store. It might also be something specific coming up, like the possibility of seeing him or her at an upcoming mutual friend's wedding.

Play through this scenario in your imagination as if you were watching it on a big movie screen in a theater, watching yourself in the film. Remember, you're going to play out a movie of this scenario where you're in complete control of how you act and what you say, and everything is going to go well and work out perfectly for you.

Play through the movie in your mind's eye, and see yourself acting calmly and confidently. Imagine what you would say out loud, how you would hold yourself, how you would respond to whatever your ex might say or do.

Give the mind movie a definite ending—a getaway line that you can use to excuse yourself easily. If your mind movie is about running into them at the grocery store, your getaway line might be something like, "Well, I really have to get to my shopping. It was nice to see you, have a good day!" At the end of the encounter, see yourself walking away from the situation feeling great about how well you handled it.

After you play through your mind movie, notice how good it feels to be in control of the encounter. Running into your ex can be uncomfortable, but it can also be empowering to know that you can handle it and that you are in control.

Take a moment now to run through at least one mind movie, then in your breakthrough journal, take a few minutes to write out your reflections on the experience.

Unhealthy or Abusive Relationships

Unhealthy or abusive relationships are all too common in the world today. If you have experienced one, it can be incredibly painful, and the pain can sometimes last after the relationship has ended.

If you suspect you've been in an unhealthy or abusive relationship, it's important for you to take time to talk to a therapist or other professional about what you've experienced. If you're unsure, there are some warning signs that can signify a possibly abusive relationship. You may have experienced some or all of the following, so make a mark next to any of these dynamics that you've experienced:

- Walking on eggshells
- Confusing behavior
- Contradictions
- Lies
- A slow erosion of confidence and self-esteem
- Increasing self-doubt
- Heightened anxiety when your partner is around
- Withdrawal from friends and family
- Living a double life behind closed doors
- Coping with an addiction
- Emotional, verbal, and/or physical abuse

If you have experienced any of these or if you know your relationship was unhealthy or abusive, first let's be clear—it wasn't your fault. It can be all too easy for victims of these dynamics to take on the blame of what happened, but you're never to blame for your partner's abusive behavior.

People stay in these sorts of relationships for a variety of reasons. Some of these might be true for you:

- You thought it was your fault
- You believed you were the problem
- You lacked the confidence to leave
- You thought you still loved your partner
- Financial reasons

- For the children and family unit
- Fear of your partner's reaction
- You saw no way out

If you do believe that you were in an abusive or unhealthy relationship, there are some specific strategies for you to take on. Again, it's vital that you discuss these issues with a therapist or other professional; they'll be able to help you evaluate what you went through, and can recommend any other specific courses of action that will help you move forward.

In general, here are some strategies for you to take on if you find yourself in this boat:

- Research their specific behaviors to see if they might have a personality disorder. There are books, tests online, and experts you could speak to.

- Getting clarity about their behavior will help you realize that, truly, none of it was your fault. This will also help reassure you that you are not going crazy!

- Set clear boundaries with your ex, including access to your home, what information you share with him or her, and when and where he or she can see any children the two of you might share.

- Keep communication to a minimum, and where possible, keep a record of it.

- Keep a diary of any unacceptable behavior with dates and details of what happened.

- Find a local domestic abuse charity that can support you.

Coping with Your Ex When You Have Children Together

If you and your ex have children together, you'll find yourself in a situation where you'll have more contact with him or her than you otherwise might want.

The guiding idea that I want you to take forward if you're in a situation like this is functionally friendly.

Functionally friendly is the strategy to use when you have to deal with your ex but are struggling to do so. Being functionally friendly will allow you to interact with your ex in a way that's best for your children and will create the smoothest possible encounters between the two of you.

The strategy is simple: in any encounter with your ex, or when you're talking with your children about your ex, set aside any issues between the two of you and *focus on your ex's positive attributes.* This doesn't mean you forget about any problems with him or your relationship. Nor does it mean that the two of you have to become good friends, or even that you have to forgive what's happened. It's simply about putting any issues aside *when* you're interacting with him or your children. This creates the foundation for a workable relationship, which is in the best interests of your children.

Shifting from parenting children together to parenting children by yourself can be a daunting transition. Whether you and your ex are sharing custody, or whether you'll be doing all the parenting moving forward, single parenting can be a challenge, especially in the beginning. You can use the tools and strategies you learn throughout this book to help empower yourself. Focus on these three positive truths:

- You now get to parent your children the way *you* choose, without anyone interfering while they're with you.

- You get quality one-on-one time with your kids.
- Your children will inspire a strength in you that you never knew you had.

If you are sharing custody or co-parenting, there are some additional strategies for you to take on, to set yourself up for success and peace of mind:

- Have clear communication with your ex about access times—avoid any ambiguity or confusion.
- Don't bad-mouth the other parent to your children.
- Always do right by your children, and wherever possible, prioritize their needs and well-being.

One of the most challenging aspects of co-parenting is dealing with the times when your kids are with your ex and you are alone, whether that's for the day, a weekend, or a month. If you're finding it hard to cope with your kids' time with your ex, here are some tips to follow:

- Plan *your* time in advance, so that you stay busy when the kids are away.
- Plan to have somewhere to go the minute your children have left.
- Use this time to move forward positively with your new life. You could take up a new hobby, learn a new skill, go to the gym, go on a few dates, etc.
- When the kids are away, focus on *you* and not your children.

Day 14

Reaching Goals
with Stepping Stones

When you're working through a breakup, so much of your life gets hurled into the unknown.

Relationships provide a sense of stability—you know who you'll be spending time with, you know what kind of activities the two of you do together, you know what your normal week looks like around that relationship.

Now that that relationship is gone, you've probably lost a lot of clarity there. Suddenly so much of what you've taken for granted is up in the air. It might be something relatively small like no longer having set dinner plans every Friday night on what used to be your date night, or it might be something major, like moving out and living in a brand-new apartment in a new part of town.

This can be scary. I know; I've been there too, but this part of a split is also a great chance to start redesigning your life to fit how *you* want it to look. You have the chance to strap yourself in to the driver's seat of your life and create the compelling future that you've only ever dreamed of.

Today, I'm going to share with you an invaluable tool I've created to help you regain control and focus and start creating this amazing new future today. It is called stepping stones.

Imagine you need to cross a stream, but can't swim or can't get your clothes wet. It might seem impossible at first; you can't just levitate over, and it's too far to just jump in one giant leap, but then you realize that someone laid out a path of stepping stones. There's a series of stones, just a small distance apart, from one side of the stream to another. Now, you're able to take the journey one step at a time—one stone at a time—across the stream. What seemed impossible is now manageable—even easy.

That's the idea with the stepping stones exercise. Identify the big goals in your life; the goals that are going to create the compelling future you dream of. Then lay out a path of steps to make that journey possible, one stone at a time. Before you know it, you'll be on the other side of the stream, living your dream life.

Stepping Stones

Let's start laying out this new path. Turn to a new page in your breakthrough journal. First, you're going to spend five minutes brainstorming all the things you would like to have, to be, or to do in your future.

Don't hold back and don't start judging whether or not something is possible or whether you know how to accomplish it. This is where you get to just let the dreams flow. Some goals might be to travel to a new country, to get yourself in the best shape of your life, or to start a new hobby you've always been interested in—anything that would be part of your dream life; your compelling future.

Take five minutes now to brainstorm these in your breakthrough journal. Now that you have that list of future goals, choose three that you would most like to create in your life; the three that most excite you. Circle them.

Take the first of those three goals and write it at the top of a blank page. Write down three small steps you can take—concrete action steps—to move closer to that goal. It's important here for you to make each step a small action step that you can understand exactly how to do.

Let's say a goal you've chosen is to become a great salsa dancer. If you've never danced before, that's a big leap to make all at once, so we're going to break it down. Your first stepping stone action might be, "Search online and make a list of salsa-dancing classes in the area." That's a simple, clear step—and it's something that doesn't feel overwhelming. Your next step might be "Pick one of those classes from the list." Again, a small and simple step. Your third step might be, "Call the school or instructor and ask about schedules and class costs."

Each stepping stone is a clear, manageable step, and for now, only focus on the first three steps. Don't worry about figuring out the whole journey from "Can't dance" to "Salsa-dancing superstar."

Repeat on a new page this step for each of the three goals you circled.

Now, we get to start putting one foot in front of the other, and walking on your new stepping stones towards your compelling future.

For each of the three goals you've identified, set a deadline of when you commit to taking the first action. As you move forward with the process, you'll want to start setting deadlines for more than one step at a time, but for now, just focus on that first step in each goal.

With these deadlines, you're going to ensure that you continue to build momentum towards your goals, step by step, day by day.

Let's take our example of becoming a great salsa dancer. The first step was to search online and find some possible classes in the area. This is a simple step and won't take too much time. Is it something you could commit to doing by the end of the day? If not today, maybe by tomorrow?

Take a moment now to write deadlines that you'll commit to, for each first step in your three goals.

Pick out at least one step that you can accomplish *today*— maybe even something that you can do right now.

As soon as you accomplish one of your stepping stone actions, check off that item as complete, write in a new action step ahead of you, and set a new deadline for your that step.

Let's say that you've researched online and have a list of dance classes in the area. Fabulous! We get to check that step off as complete.

The next two steps are, "Pick one of those classes from the list," then "Call the school or instructor and ask about schedules and costs." We always want to have at least three stepping stones, so it's time to write a new one. What will your next step be after you call the school? Maybe "Pick out a date to start a first class."

Set a new deadline that you'll commit to for the next step in front of you, so write in a deadline for "Pick one of those classes from the list."

With this exercise, you'll always be moving forward to your compelling future, while keeping things manageable. This helps you avoid the overwhelming task of trying to figure everything out at once, and you build tangible momentum, day after day.

As you get comfortable with this first stage, you can start adding new goals or planning out more than three steps at a time, but for now, start with just these three goals, three steps each.

Part of the benefit of this step-by-step breakdown is that you get to celebrate each step taken. Did you accomplish that first small step? Awesome, you get to celebrate! Another small step? Another accomplishment to pat yourself on the back for.

You're going to soon see your pages filling up with checkmarks and smiley-faces of steps you've accomplished. Before you know it, you're going to be hitting those big goals and living the compelling future you've dreamed of.

Day 15

The Carrot and the Stick— Understanding What Motivates You

As we focus on creating your compelling future, it's important to have clarity on what motivates you.

Remember back on day three when we focused on your map of the world? The patterns and habits and assumptions that you learned in large part from the people and things and events around you? We're going to focus today on part of that map— your continent of motivation.

All human beings are motivated by two things—pain and pleasure. You might have heard of the carrot-and-stick metaphor. The idea is that if you're riding a horse and you want it to move forward, you could motivate it either by dangling a carrot in front of it, or whacking it with a stick from behind.

If you're more motivated by pleasure, it's the carrot that's most able to propel you forward; if you're more motivated by pain, it's the stick that's most potent.

Now, both pain and pleasure are always able to motivate us to some degree. You might be more of a pain-motivated person, but if there's a pile of money sitting in your front yard, you can bet you'll be motivated to go grab it! Conversely, you might be more of a pleasure-motivated person, but the pain of your hand on a hot stove is definitely still going to motivate you to pull your hand away.

The idea here is that each of us tends to be motivated *more* by one or the other, and it's going to be important for you to know which drives you more.

Imagine you're trying to lose some weight, and you want to give yourself an extra boost of motivation to keep up with your exercise and nutrition plan. If you're more of a pleasure-motivated person, you might want to put up a photo on your fridge of you when you were at your fittest and healthiest. Seeing that picture of what you're striving towards, the pleasurable goal ahead of you, will motivate you to keep moving forward. On the other hand, if you're more of a pain-motivated person, you might find it more useful to put up a photo on the fridge of you at your heaviest and most unhealthy; that image of the pain you're steering away *from* will keep you motivated.

Now, put yourself in this scenario. Which do you think would motivate you more? This will give you a big clue as to whether you're primarily a pleasure-motivated or pain-motivated person.

It's also important to understand that if you try to use the motivation style that *doesn't* fit you, it can backfire on you.

In the example above, those who are primarily pleasure-motivated are only going to sabotage themselves by putting up photos of them at their most unhealthy weight. When they see that picture, they'll only feel worse about things. Their focus will be on the pain, and so they'll lose motivation; they might even find themselves eating junk food to deal with the stress of the picture on the fridge.

On the flip side, someone who is primarily pain-motivated might not be served well by a picture of them looking their best on the fridge. If they're unhealthily overweight, but have a photo of them looking great on the fridge, they might lose the motivation to change things, and become even more complacent with how things currently are.

Which side of the fence do you fall on? Pull out your breakthrough journal, and free-write for at least five minutes about what motivates you. Think back on when you've had goals in the past, and what motivated you the most then. When you were in school, were you motivated by the goal of getting a good grade or the fear or getting in trouble or failing? In your work, are you more motivated by the pleasure of praise and raises or the pain of reprimands and looming deadlines?

After writing about what has motivated you in the past, identify whether you're more pleasure- or pain-motivated.

A Word of Caution About Pain Motivation

As with so much on this journey, there is no right or wrong answer here. There's nothing inherently better about being motivated more by the carrot or the stick. It's all about what works best for *you*, but a word of caution here. If you're primarily motivated by pain, there's a particular pitfall that you'll need to watch out for. When someone is more motivated by pleasure, their primary drive is to move *towards* what they want; on the other hand, when someone is more motivated by pain, their primary drive is to move *away from* what they don't want.

The danger is that for pain-motivated individuals, it can be tempting to simply jump into *anything* different, to get away from that source of pain. When it comes to moving forward from a split, sometimes that can turn into jumping into any new relationship to run from the pain of the last one.

Unfortunately, that new relationship is usually just as bad or even worse than the one you're running from. I've seen this pattern in this history of many clients I've worked with.

If you've identified that you're primarily motivated by pain, that's perfectly fine; just know that you'll have to keep an extra careful eye on what you're moving *towards*, as well as what you're moving away from.

And don't worry—following the steps and strategies in this 30-day plan is going to have you clear on the amazing future that you're launching into.

Day 16

The Five Love Languages

When we talk about love, we all know what we're referring to. Even if it's sometimes hard to describe, we can all bring to mind that special blend of adoration, compassion, dedication, and giddy infatuation, but guess what? Even though we're all able to experience love, we don't all express or receive love in the same ways.

A few years back, I was working with a couple, Kendrick and Monica. It was clear to me from the outside than the two of them loved each other dearly, but both of them came to me saying that they felt unloved in their relationship. On top of that, neither of them could understand how the other could possibly feel unloved.

Monica described how she would start each day telling Kendrick that she loved him. Before they left separately for work, she would be sure to tell him again. Throughout the day, she'd text him a simple I-love-you message, to make sure he never went long without hearing it, but still, Kendrick felt unloved.

Kendrick told me how he would always go out of his way to show Monica how much he loved her. He would make sure that he woke up first, to get breakfast started and bring Monica a mug of tea when she woke up. Every weekend, Kendrick would clean out Monica's car, inside and out. He'd be sure to pick up groceries whenever they needed it, and he always volunteered to be the one to do the dishes or clean the bathroom, yet despite all of this, Monica felt unloved.

Monica couldn't understand how Kendrick could feel unloved—she told him that she loved him all the time. When Kendrick would say, "But those are just words," Monica would feel frustrated and helpless. To Monica, all of Kendrick's actions to help out were just nice things he did, but didn't do anything about her feeling unloved; this made Kendrick feel unappreciated and powerless.

What was the issue? The two of them had different *love languages* and didn't realize it.

The Five Love Languages

You may have heard the term love languages before. It was coined in 1995 by Gary Chapman in his wildly popular book, *The Five Love Languages*.

The idea here is that there are five main ways that people express and receive love. For each person, there are one or two ways that are their primary love languages—the ways that they most readily express their love for others, or experience love coming from others.

The five languages are:

1. *Words of affirmation*—verbalized, spoken love; a simple "I love you," or someone telling you how much you mean to them, or giving you verbal encouragement, etc.
2. *Acts of service*—love expressed through actions; doing favors for someone or doing tasks to make their lives easier or more enjoyable.
3. *Physical affection*—love expressed through touch; hugs, kisses, sexual intimacy, holding hands, even a touch on the shoulder.

4. *Quality time*—love expressed through shared moments; making time to be fully present with someone, whether just for a few minutes in the morning or a full date night.
5. *Gifts*—love expressed through tangible presents; tokens that show you were on someone's mind—not necessarily expensive presents; this could be as simple as a quick, handwritten note on the mirror in the morning.

Kendrick's primary love language was acts of service, while Monica's primary love language was words of affirmation. When a partner isn't speaking the love language that you hear, it leaves you feeling unloved, even if they are deeply in love with you and doing their best to show it in the way natural to them. This is what was happening with Kendrick and Monica.

The good news is that we can learn to speak new love languages so that our partners can hear it. When Monica described specifically what would have her feel loved, Kendrick was more than happy to take it on and vice versa.

Understanding how the different love languages operate, and especially becoming clear on *your* primary love language, will be a vital tool to creating thriving, love-filled relationships in your future. It can also be helpful to creating clarity about why past relationships fell apart.

It's also important to realize that each person has certain rules about what counts in their love language. For me, words of affirmation are my number-one language. In a relationship, I need to hear that I'm loved in words, but it goes deeper than that; I need to hear it x number of times a day. It doesn't really count if you just say it after I say it, and so on. It might sound silly, but this is just how human beings are wired.

When you're clear on your own love-language needs, you're able to communicate those needs to a future partner and feel the love you deserve.

Once you're clear on your one or two most prevalent love languages, pull out your breakthrough journal and spend a few minutes writing out answers to the following questions:

1. What are your primary love languages?
2. What specifically in these languages makes you feel loved?
3. Thinking back, what do you think your most recent ex's love language was? Any past exes?

How can you use this information to improve your relationships in the future?

Day 17

Understanding
Your Communication Styles

Yesterday, we focused on different love languages and how you most readily receive and give love, but when it comes to any relationship, there's a lot of communication outside of just communicating love—and just as with love, there are many communication styles that people have learned from different maps of the world.

Today, we're going to broaden our view into these other areas of relationships. I once found myself working with a couple, Louis and Caitlyn. Their relationship was on the ropes; it didn't take me long to realize that the crux of their issues was how the two of them separately dealt with conflict. In their relationship, the slightest disagreement or smallest conflict would quickly devolve into pain and hurt feelings without any resolution. Louise and Caitlyn clearly loved each other, and they both knew that the other loved them, but they couldn't seem to find a way out of any conflict.

The reason? They had different communication styles and didn't even realize it.

Louis had grown up in a household of big personalities and loud voices. When his parents—or anyone else in his extended family—had a disagreement or conflict, they would shout it out.

They would stay in the room together, yelling out their feelings and opinions, hands gesticulating wildly. Eventually, they would come to understand each other's point of view and work out a solution to the problem. Both of Louis's parents dealt with conflict in this way, so it worked for them.

Things looked quite a bit different in Caitlyn's household when she was growing up. Both of Caitlyn's parents were quiet and reserved, and so when an argument started, they would hit the pause button. Each of them would go off to cool down and think things through; later on, they'd come back together and talk things out at the kitchen table. Both of Caitlyn's parents dealt with conflict like this, so it worked for them.

But now, Louis and Caitlyn had grown up and fallen in love with each other, and each of them still had the communication style they'd learned from their parents. You can probably guess what happened next.

When an argument or conflict would arise, Louis would want to stick with it and yell things out until a solution was reached. Caitlyn would want to leave the room to cool down for a bit until they could talk things over calmly and quietly to create resolution. When Louis would want to yell it out in the moment, Caitlyn only felt attacked and like she wasn't given any space to think things over. When Caitlyn wanted to leave the room and cool off, Louis felt like he was being abandoned and like Caitlyn didn't actually care about the relationship.

What's so important to realize here is that *neither of them was wrong*—they just had learned different styles.

Louis's parents' style worked for them because they were on the same page; Caitlyn's parents' style worked for them because they were on the same page. The problem that Louis and Caitlyn faced was that they were both trying to live out different communication styles, not realizing that the other had a different map of the world.

When Louis and Caitlyn understood what was happening, they were able to create a plan for resolving conflict that took into account both of their needs. When things did fall off the rails, they were able to bring their understanding to bear—they knew it wasn't that the other person didn't care about them; they simply had a different map of the world.

Understanding Your Relationship Communication Styles

As you move forward and start thinking about creating thriving, loving relationships in the future, it's important for you to understand your own relationship communication styles. This also has the benefit of bringing clarity to past relationships and making sense of why things didn't work.

I want you to take out your breakthrough journal and write about your own communication styles. There are a few questions for you to consider:

1. What communication styles do I default to?
2. Where did I learn these communication styles?
3. Where did my past relationships have breakdowns due to different communication styles?

Since we focused yesterday on different styles of communicating love, consider some of these areas of communication today:

- Resolving conflict
- Apologies
- Expressing needs
- Talking about the past/future

Understanding Others Outside of Just Romance

As with so much of our work here, you're building skills that will benefit your whole life, not simply in romantic partnerships.

When you understand that different people have different communication styles, you can start to employ this knowledge everywhere in life. Does your boss have a different style of conflict-resolution than you do? If that creates tension, how can you use this knowledge to further yourself at work? What about with your friends, or family? If you have kids, even your own children, whose map of the world you've helped create, might easily have a different communication style than you.

When you learn how to understand and work through different communication styles, the benefits and breakthroughs will start appearing everywhere in life.

Day 18

Transforming Your Limiting Beliefs

Ready to hear something really wild?

There's an insidious group of things—some trouble-making little gremlins—that are holding you back more than anything else in life. They're inside your head; you can get rid of them if you choose to, but you *probably don't even know they're there.*

They're your limiting beliefs.

Think back to your map of the world, which we talked about back on day three. Your map of the world defines how you think about the world, how you interact with people, what you value, and how you think about yourself. You learn most of it at a very young age—from about infancy to seven years old—and then it's just a bunch of programs and patterns running in the background. Like a fish that doesn't realize it's in water because it's all the fish has ever known, your map of the world colors everything you see and every moment you live, whether you realize it or not.

Part of that is your set of limiting beliefs. Your limiting beliefs are the core assumptions you have about yourself, how others see you, and your place in the world. They often hold you back because they prevent you from doing or saying things that would challenge them.

What does that look like? One of the most common limiting beliefs I encounter is the belief, "I'm just not good enough."

Maybe that belief is something that first came from childhood, or maybe it's something that sprang up in your breakup, but if you're operating under that limiting belief, it's going to hold you back. As you move forward after a split, you might avoid dating again or asking out someone you fancy because in the background there's that I'm-just-not-good-enough mantra. Maybe you avoid speaking up in workplace meetings or asking your boss for a raise, again, because of that I'm-just-not-good-enough limiting belief.

Now, here's the kicker: limiting beliefs do not necessarily represent what is true or factual; just what you believe. More often than not, they're completely wrong, from a fact-based view.

What makes limiting beliefs so tricky is that, because we act in ways that assume they're true, we start building up evidence to back them up. Maybe you never ask for a raise at work because you have that not-good-enough limiting belief, but then your brain tells you, "See! Your boss isn't giving you a raise because you're just not good enough. Told you so."

If you're having trouble recovering after a split, there are probably some limiting beliefs in your way. You might be operating with some common ones, like:

- "I'm just not lovable and no one will love me again."
- "I'm not strong enough to rebuild my life."
- "Nothing is ever going to go right for me."
- "I'm weak and powerless."
- "I'm destined to be sad and alone."

Limiting beliefs hold you back from living the life of your dreams, but there's good news too—if you face them head on, you can get rid of them and replace them with what serves you.

That's what today is all about—breaking down your limiting beliefs and starting to replace them with empowering ones. First, we get to identify what particular limiting beliefs are operating in the background of *your* life.

Take out your breakthrough journal and spend five or ten minutes free-writing your answers to each of these two questions:

1. Where are your results not in alignment with what you really want to be, do, or have?
2. What area of your life have you really tried to improve, but no matter what, things just don't get better?

After you've written your responses to those questions, go back and read over what you've written. Now is where you get to really dive under the surface. What are the limiting beliefs you have about yourself that might be holding you back in these areas?

Try to boil things down to "I am…" or "I'm not…" statements. Things like "I am always going to be alone" or "I'm not physically attractive." These "I am" and "I'm not" statements are the beliefs that are at the core of what hold you back.

On a new page, write out the limiting beliefs that you're able to identify.

Getting Rid of and Replacing Your Limiting Beliefs

Now we're getting to the really juicy part. One by one, we're going to bust up your limiting beliefs and replace them with new, empowering beliefs that will propel you towards the life of your dreams.

On a new page in your Breakthrough Journal, write the first limiting belief that you identified.

Next, you get to acknowledge that although this is your current *belief*, it is not actually the truth. Take a few minutes to write down evidence from your life that goes against this belief.

For example, if you have the limiting belief of "I'm unattractive," you might write down, "People have told me they find me attractive," or "I matched with four new people on

Tinder last week," or, "I caught someone checking me out at the coffee shop yesterday."

After you've compiled evidence against your limiting belief, it's time to pick a new one with which to replace it. Pick a limiting belief that is in some way the empowering opposite of your limiting belief. For instance, you might choose to replace "I'm unattractive" with "I'm beautiful and attractive exactly as I am right now."

Now we get to start cementing that empowering belief into your consciousness. Write down three steps that you can take today to start making this new belief a reality. This might include a sticky note on your bathroom mirror with the belief written on it, or repeating it in the morning as a new mantra, or taking an action that puts the belief into motion.

You might be skeptical at this point that little steps like these could have such a profound impact. That's understandable. But remember, it's about dialing down—bit by bit—the negative impact that this limiting belief has had on your life. Freeing yourself from its grip is accomplished in little steps, every day.

Now, you get to repeat this with all of the other limiting beliefs you identified. Part of what's so great here is that *you have control* over the beliefs you operate with. When you're overrun with limiting beliefs, they hold you back without you even realizing it. When you put in the work to replace those limiting beliefs with empowering beliefs, the new ones will start pushing you forward without you even realizing it.

Before you know it, things in your life will start to just come together in amazing ways, and the life you dream of will start unfolding right in front of you.

Limiting Beliefs Regarding Breakups and Children

I want to bring attention here to one particularly insidious limiting belief that I see in so many of my clients who have shared children with their ex.

That limiting belief is some form of: "The breakup is going to be traumatic to our kids." This idea comes up so often in our culture. We hear of couples staying together "for the kids"—as if it's in the children's best interest to watch their parents suffer through a relationship that isn't working. We hear of broken homes and the trauma that divorce or parental splits can cause for children.

Let's be honest here. If you have children with your ex, will the split be a challenge for those kids? Sure, but challenge doesn't mean trauma, and in fact, in just the same way the challenge of your split can be a golden opportunity for *you*, so can it also be a golden opportunity for your children.

If your kids are going through this breakup with you, you're setting a powerful example for them. They're learning from you, right now, how to handle the tough curveballs that life sometimes throws at us.

Just by the fact that you're reading this book and putting these techniques into practice, I can tell that you're facing this challenge with tenacity and compassion, and with a strong intention to move forward and better yourself. And guess what?! *That's what you're teaching your kids. Whether you like it or not you are their role model and they are learning from you.*

Life is going to present challenges to your children. They will face disappointment, someone will let them down, they may not get the job they want, someone will lie to them; and right now, they're looking to you and learning how to turn crisis into opportunity. They're learning how to face challenges head-on and how to grow through them. They're learning what it looks like to be committed to creating a fantastic, happy, thriving life. They are learning that it is not what happens to you in life that defines you; it's what you do about it that makes you the person you are. When things don't go the way they want, they will remember what they've learned from you and be able to dust themselves off and carry on. They will believe and know that this is possible—because you've shown them that by example.

And that is a powerful and extremely valuable life-lesson for them to learn. The split might be a challenge for them right now, but because you're committed to turning your own breakup into breakthrough, you're creating breakthroughs for your children, and that is a gift beyond measure.

Day 19

The Secret Weapon
for Dissolving Conflict

Over the last week, we've been looking at tools and insights to help you avoid conflict and breakdowns, both in moving forward through your split and in preparing yourself for future thriving relationships, but I've got some real-talk for you: conflicts will still arise. Conflicts between people are always just going to be part of life. Looking forward towards a future relationship? There will at times be conflict. Still dealing in some way with your ex? Maybe you have children together and are navigating that journey? There will be conflict from time to time there.

What I'm going to share with you today is a tool that will prove absolutely invaluable. The first time you put it into practice, you will be shocked at how transformative it is. This is my secret weapon for dissolving conflict.

Shoe Shifting

Welcome to shoe shifting.

The idea here is simple—you're going to step into the shoes of three different people and simply describe the conflict. At the end of this shifting, you'll be amazed at the insight and understanding you've gained, as well at how deeply transformed your feelings about the conflict are.

It's important to note here that this technique is *not* appropriate for things like trauma or abuse. This is for everyday sorts of conflicts or disagreements—arguments about the small-but-important things in life—the sorts of conflict that might start around something small but can boil into furious arguments.

The exercise is as simple as the idea, and you're going to learn it by putting it into practice in your breakthrough journal.

On a new page, write out a conflict that you currently have negative energy on; some conflict that is causing you grief. If you're still having contact with your ex, it might be something with him or her. If not, you can pick any other conflict you're in the midst of right now—maybe with someone at work or a friend or family member.

At the top of the page, write out a description of the conflict—just a simple one-sentence summary of what's going on. Now, the first shoes you're going to put on are some familiar ones: your own. From your point of view, you're first going to write out answers to the following questions:

- What are you seeing?
- What are you hearing?
- What are you feeling?
- What are you thinking?

Take at least a few minutes now to write out your side of the disagreement—what you're seeing, hearing, feeling, and thinking in this conflict—all from your point of view. This is probably familiar ground for you to cover, but let's get it all down on the page.

After you've completed that, you're going to do your first shoe-shifting by stepping into the shoes of whoever you're having this conflict with. If you're working through a conflict with your ex, this is where you put yourself in his or her shoes.

What am I talking about, really, when I say "in their shoes?"

You're going to try to look at this situation through their eyes. As you do so, keep in mind all the tools of understanding you've gained over these last couple weeks. You're going to imagine this situation with this person's map of the world. To whatever extent you can, you're going to think about what this must be like for them—with that person's limiting beliefs, communication styles, baggage, and so on.

Now, you're going to answer those same four questions about this conflict—*as that person.* As that person, what are you seeing? Hearing? Feeling? Thinking?

Take at least five minutes to argue this from his or her point of view. Write out your answers to these questions from this other person's point of view. Remember, you're writing *as* them, so you'll still want to use I/me/my language. This might seem like a minor detail, but that minor language detail will do a lot to put you right in this person's shoes.

Next, you're going to shift into the shoes of a trusted third party; someone who knows you, knows the person you're in conflict with, and whom the both of you trust. This might be a fellow coworker, an advisor, or another family member—whatever feels right for this particular situation.

Now, you're going to answer those same questions, from this trusted third party's perspective. Imagine that you and the person you're in conflict with have both told this third person your sides of the story. You're going to do your best to adopt this third person's map of the world, beliefs, perspectives, and so on.

Take at least five minutes again to answer the same four questions about this conflict. What are you seeing? Hearing? Feeling? Thinking? And again, use "I/me/my" language, from that trusted third party's shoes.

And that's it—simple, but hugely powerful.

On a new page, take a few minutes to write how your perspective on this conflict has changed or expanded. Describe also how your feelings about the conflict have changed. What emotions have you dialed down? What emotions have you dialed up?

This tool is one of my favorites to demonstrate at group workshops because people are shocked at the transformation they see on stage in just a few minutes.

I remember at one of my workshops, I was on stage teaching this exercise with a woman named Gillian.

Gillian and her ex, Wade, had split earlier that year, when Wade left her for a new woman. He and Gillian had a son together and conflicts kept erupting between them as they navigated co-parenting. One particular issue had Gillian absolutely steaming-mad: a new desk. As Gillian told it in her first step of the shoe-shifting exercise, her son was in need of a new desk. She and Wade agreed that Wade would pay for it, as part of splitting the costs of parenting. Gillian picked out a particular desk that would fit with their son's décor, as well as physically fit perfectly in the spot she'd prepared for it. She sent the link to Wade for him to order. Weeks went by without any desk and Gillian kept reaching out to Wade about it, asking him if he'd ordered it yet. Finally, weeks later, the new desk arrived at Gillian's house, but it wasn't the desk she'd picked out. It didn't match the new furniture, and didn't even fit where she'd planned to put it. When she called Wade to confront him about it, she found out that not only did he indeed order a different desk—his new girlfriend had been the one to pick it out.

Gillian was furious about this. When she told the story on stage at the workshop, over a month had passed, but she was still shaking with anger by the end of telling her version of events. Clearly, it was about more than just the desk. Gillian described how she felt completely belittled and ignored, how she felt Wade was trying to make his new girlfriend the decision-maker when it came to *her* son, and how frustrated she was when she thought about having to deal with this kind of thing for years to come.

On stage, I told Gillian to stand up from the chair she'd been sitting in. I told her that when she sat back down, she would be in Wade's shoes and would tell us what happened from his perspective. "Ugh, I don't even want to be inside his head for a second," Gillian groaned, but I urged her to give it a shot, and she relented.

She sat back down, and started telling the story again.

"Well," she said, slowly at first then picking up speed, "I've never been good about getting stuff like this handled. I have a bad habit of forgetting little tasks like ordering stuff we need. I know I do it, and it stresses me out, but I just procrastinate and forget things. I kept forgetting to order the desk for weeks, and I felt really guilty about it. When I finally went online to order it, the desk that Gillian had picked out was out of stock. I felt awful. My girlfriend is good at interior design, she's a real estate agent, and I'm no good at that stuff, so I asked her advice. She picked out one that she thought would work, and I ordered it. I thought Gillian would be happy that I ordered a good replacement, but she was just furious, which only made me upset, because I always feel like nothing I do is good enough for her."

When Gillian finished her retelling, she had a shocked look on her face.

"Ok great," I said. "Now one more time, from a trusted third party."

Gillian started telling the story again, from the perspective of their son's teacher. "It's clear to me," she said, "that both Gillian and Wade are making Seth a priority here. They both care about his schooling, and are both trying to do their best when it comes to this new co-parenting arrangement. They're both holding onto a lot of baggage from their relationship, and it makes it hard for them to communicate about things. I think it's clear how much they love Seth though, and that he's what matters most to them."

By the end of the shoe shifting, Gillian was laughing at how angry she'd been. After just a few minutes, all her anger evaporated—and that anger had been boiling for *weeks*. Right then and there, she texted Wade to apologize for being so upset, and thanked him for making the effort to get Seth a great desk.

That's the power of shoe shifting. It can take all the negative energy around a conflict—even if that conflict and energy have been boiling for a long time—and just dissolve it all.

The next time you get stuck in a conflict or start to feel those negative feelings building up around a conflict, just pull out this secret weapon and fire away.

Day 20

Change How You Feel, In A Heartbeat—Physiology

Don't you wish you could change how you feel, in a heartbeat? Well, luckily, you can.

Remember, there's no magic wand to instantly go from a level-10 sadness straight to a level-zero sadness, but there are strategies for dialing up and down your different emotions, and over the next three days I'm going to share with you the trifecta of ways to change your mood—and the tools that go with each.

There are three key areas that allow you to do some serious dialing-down and dialing-up almost instantly: physiology, language, and focus. Today we're going to focus our attention on the physiology corner of the triangle.

Physiology is all about the physical state of your body. For our purposes, we're going to deal with the physical states of your body that you can control—your body language and facial language.

It's no shocker that your mood affects your body and facial language. At its simplest, we all know that when we're happy we tend to smile, and when we're sad we tend to frown. You're probably to some extent familiar with some common body language patterns beyond that. Maybe you know that when we're sad we tend to lean forward and hunch our shoulders, and when we're happy or confident we tend to arch our back straighter and hold our shoulders back, opening up our chest.

Here's the real kicker, though. Our brains are funny things. They're wired to automatically change our body postures and facial expressions to respond to our moods, but that wiring goes both ways—meaning that you can change your mood simply by physically changing how you hold your body and face.

When you think about it, that's a pretty weird feature of the human body, but it's true, and since it is, we're going to take full advantage of it.

Using Your Physiology to Shift Your Mood

To start, here's a quick-and-easy demonstration of how this works. Put a smile on your face; a big smile that stretches all the way up to your eyes. Hold it for five or 10 seconds, and notice how it shifts your mood and emotional experience right now.

Isn't that wild?

Studies have shown that simply having participants hold a pencil long-ways between their teeth has a substantial impact on their mood—simply because it has them hold their faces in a way that is *similar* to a smile. The study participants weren't told to smile, and didn't even know it was a study about the effect of facial language on mood, and still the simple act had a measurable impact.

If even an almost-smile can have a positive impact on someone's mood, imagine the potency of what you can create here!

The ways you can bio-hack your mood through your physiology are near endless, but we're going to start with mood-shifting between two particular moods: going from one that you don't want to experience to one that you do.

Pick a negative state of mind that you want to dial down in your life; maybe something like sadness, anxiety, or fear—

105

whatever you feel you're particularly struggling with. Next, pick a positive state of mind that you'd like to shift your negative mood into; maybe happiness or excitement.

Identify the particular body language and facial characteristics that these states of mind correlate to for you. There are some commonalities across different people, but everyone is unique, with their own unique physiology. We want to identify what is going to be most potent for you.

In a moment you're going to put this book down, stand up, and put yourself in that negative state of mind—-don't worry, we'll shift out of it soon! Choose a negative state that you experience a lot and want to shift. Let that feeling wash over you and allow your body to move how it wants. Once you're in the middle of it, I want you to bring your attention to your body and face, and identify as many characteristics as you can. How are you holding your face and head? Your shoulders? Your back, arms, and legs? Do a whole-body scan. If you can, do this in front of a mirror or with a friend to identify as many features as you can. Write all these features in your breakthrough journal.

After you've gone through that process, it's time to identify the features for the positive state of mind. Go through the same process here—bring yourself into that state of mind; notice what your body and face is doing, then write down as many physiological features as you can identify.

Now, here's the fun part. Practice jumping from the negative mood into the positive mood, by shifting your body language. Stand up again and drop into that negative state of mind, letting your body adopt the related physiology; then change your body and facial language into what you identified with the positive state of mind; see how quickly you can shift into that mood.

Take at least a few minutes now to practice moving your body and mind back and forth between these two states, paying attention to the positive shifts in your state of mind as you shift into the positive-mood physiology. The more you practice this, the easier it will be for you to put into action in your life.

Keep in mind that you'll sometimes want to practice this out in public, where it might be awkward to jump through full-body shifts. It's useful to identify one shift that you can make that has a big impact on how you feel. This might be something like how you hold your shoulders, or your neck, or just a squeeze of your hand. When you focus on this one small thing, you can use it to shift your body language in a split-second, even when out in public. This way you have both tools in your arsenal—full-body shifting for when it's appropriate for you to practice that, and single-focus shifting that you can use anytime and anywhere.

This is one of those tools that you can practice anytime, anywhere; and with just a few simple shifts in your body, you'll be able to shift your state of mind in a heartbeat.

Day 21

Change How You Feel
In A Heartbeat—Language

Yesterday, we looked at how you can use body language and facial expressions to change how you feel in a heartbeat—almost bio-hacking your mind and body to shift your mood at will.

Today, we're going to look at another process through which we can change our mood: language.

With physiology, we took advantage of peculiar ways that our brains are wired, and again today we're going to take advantage of a funny aspect of our minds. First, I'll show you what I'm talking about.

In a moment, I'm going to ask you a question. I want you to read the question, but I *don't* want you to answer it—not even in your mind; don't even think about the answer. Just read the question and move on.

Ok—What is the country in which Paris is located?

You thought of the answer, didn't you? Even without trying to, even actively trying *not* to, you couldn't help thinking of France, even if just for a split second before you pushed the thought away.

Let's try again.

I'm going to say something in a moment, but I want you to *not* think of it. Don't picture it, even for a fraction of a second.

Ok—blue elephant.

You did it again!

This is how our brains work. If we ask a question, we can't help coming up with an answer. It might not always be the *right* answer (how much easier would school have been in that case?), but our brains are wired to come up with an answer. Similarly, our brains can't operate on negatives; if we tell ourselves not to think of something, we're going to think about it right away, then just try to shove it out.

What does this have to do with turning a breakup into breakthroughs? Well, when you're going through a painful split, your internal monologue—the little voice in your head—is probably constantly peppering you with negative thoughts and questions, even if you don't realize it.

When we ask ourselves something like, "Why wasn't I good enough for [him or her]?" our brains are going to find an answer. They just can't help it. When you ask yourself that, your brain is immediately going to say "Uh, hmm, let's see. Well, you must not be attractive; you're not very good at this; you're really crummy at that; you're no fun to be around…" and on and on.

Remember, your brain doesn't always come up with a *true* answer. Odds are, everything it will throw at you will be outright false or a wild exaggeration, but the brain doesn't worry about that; it just needs to answer the question.

These thoughts then color our entire perception of ourselves and the world. We think negative thoughts like, "I just can't do this," or "I'm going to be alone forever," ask ourselves negative questions like, "What is wrong with me?" or, "Why am I so unlovable?" and then we live in a world swimming with negativity. And the cycle repeats.

Breaking the Cycle with New Language

It's time to break that cycle and start living in a world of positivity because here's the useful part here—just like your brain will always come up with answers to *negative* questions, so will it always come up with answers to *positive* questions.

The strategy, then, is to start replacing negative thoughts and questions with positive ones. Just as negative ones create downward spirals, so will these empowering thoughts and questions begin to create a positive feedback loop. It might feel clunky at first, but soon these uplifting thoughts create a more positive outlook, and it becomes all the more natural to use this positive language, and on and on.

Let's start building this positive feedback loop for you.

In your breakthrough journal, I first want you to identify the negative questions and disempowering thoughts and words that you use a lot. Some common questions and words include:

- "What is wrong with me?"
- "What did I do to deserve this?"
- "Why don't they love me anymore?"
- never/always
- broken
- abandoned

If you're having trouble identifying the negative language that you use most often, keep a closer eye on your thoughts and spoken words the rest of the day. You'll probably notice a pattern of particular negativity. You can also ask a close friend or family member what they've been hearing from you; if it's someone you talk to regularly, they probably have a good idea of the language you use to keep yourself down.

Once you've got this list at least started, turn to a new page. Here, I want you to brainstorm some positive phrases and questions that will empower you. Some you might choose from include:

- "What's good about this right now?"

- "What am I grateful for right now?"
- "What can I do right now to make this better?"
- opportunity
- new beginning
- fresh start

Now, we get to start working this empowering language into your everyday life.

Get a pad of sticky notes and write each empowering phrase and question that you came up with onto different sticky notes. Put them up around your home where you'll see them as you go about your day; maybe one on the fridge, one on your bathroom mirror, one on your nightstand. If it's possible for you, you could even put up a few at work or in your car.

Each time you see these notes, take just a moment to focus on what they say. Before you know it, this empowering language is going to create a momentous shift in your outlook.

This language-shifting can also be used when you're feeling particularly down and want to dial-up or dial-down your emotions in a heartbeat. Just take a moment to ask yourself one of your empowering questions; your brain will kick into gear and start giving you positive answers.

Like so many of the strategies and tools in this book, this technique gets stronger the more you use it, so let's get those sticky notes up and start transforming your language.

Day 22

Change How You Feel
In A Heartbeat—Focus

We've already talked about the power of your focus—remember from day five, one of the keys to surviving and thriving was focusing on the future.

Many of the tools I've given you so far have dealt with shifting your focus. When you practice the gratitude exercise, you're shifting your focus onto gratitude. When you do shoe shifting, you're refocusing your ideas and emotions around a conflict.

Today, we're going to dive deeper into how to transform your life by transforming your focus, and we're going to use a particular psychological tool to do so: submodalities.

The Power of Submodalities

Submodalities sounds like a really technical word, but the concept is pretty simple. Submodalities are the sensation-based ways that we give meaning to experiences and memories.

We use our five senses to interpret information about the world through these submodalities:

1. *Visual submodalities*: brightness, color, shape, location, distance, contrast, focus/clarity, movement, speed, density

2. *Auditory submodalities*: volume, pitch, tempo, rhythm, timbre, duration, clarity, location, distance
3. *Kinesthetic submodalities*: pressure, location, frequency, texture, temperature, intensity, vibration
4. *Olfactory submodalities*: smells
5. *Gustatory submodalities*: tastes

We understand something like a campfire with sensory information about its heat, color, brightness, smell, and so on.

Our brains actually do a very similar thing with emotional experiences and memories; we attach submodalities to them, which then define how we interpret and feel them. Although you've probably never thought about something like, "What's the color and texture of my anger?" these submodalities play a huge role in our experience of emotions and memories. This makes them extremely powerful and effective tools to consciously change how you feel.

By changing the submodalities of your emotions and memories, you're changing the meaning of those experiences on a deep, neurological level. When we change the meaning of the experience, we change our state of mind around it. This then impacts how we respond, how we behave in new situations, and ultimately the reality we live in and our map of the world. Playing with submodalities, we're literally redefining our lives from the ground up.

If this all sounds a little wonky now, don't worry—I'm going to guide you through an exercise that puts this into action.

Putting It into Action

For this exercise, have your breakthrough journal handy for reflections. Make sure you're in a comfortable space where you know you won't be interrupted—shut the door or close your blinds, turn your phone on silent, and so on.

113

This exercise is one that some people take to easily and experience massive impact from right away. For others, this stretches their comfort zone a bit and creates subtler shifts until they get used to it. Whatever your first experience with it, I want you to give it your all. Remember, you gave your word that you would play full-out.

Ok, let's get started.

First, I want you to bring to mind a negative emotion that has a really strong hold on you, something that has been hitting you really hard lately. Maybe for you this is anger or sadness. Whatever the emotion is that you've chosen, I want you to focus on that feeling. Bring it to mind, maybe think of some memories that evoke it, until you're really feeling it.

In your breakthrough journal, I want you to write a description of this emotion using submodalities, by answering the following questions. You might also want to glance back up at the list of submodalities to help give you direction in describing the experience.

- Where specifically can you feel this in your body? (e.g., on my shoulders, in my chest, etc.)
- Is it moving, or spinning at all? How?
- What does it look like? What color/size/shape? E.g., "grey, big, and spiky"
- What does it sound like? Is there any noise associated with it?
- What does it feel like? Is there a specific texture? Temperature? Weight? E.g., "hard, cold, and heavy"
- Is there any kind of smell associated with it?
- Is there any kind of taste associated with it?

Now, we're going to use submodalities to transform what you're feeling.

Be sure you're still connected to that particular feeling; notice all the descriptions you've listed. Notice any movement, color, sound, and so on. Bring your hands to wherever that feeling is and imagine yourself grabbing hold of it. Bring your hands out in front of you, pulling out that feeling and holding it up in front of you. Next, replace all the submodalities step by step with new ones that you like and desire to feel instead:

- Change the movement or speed of the feeling—e.g., if it is spinning one way then reverse it and make it spin the other way. It is was bouncing, maybe make it still—whatever makes it feel better for you.
- Change its color to your favorite color.
- Change its noise to your favorite sounds.
- Changes its texture to a feeling that you love.
- Replace the old smell with your favorite one.
- Replace any tastes with your favorite taste.

Now, I want you to take the transformed version in your hands and pull it back inside you, right back where you got it from.

Notice the difference of what you're feeling, and in your breakthrough journal, write down what shifts you're noticing and how you're feeling now.

*   *   *

This is one of the tools that has the potential to create a radical, instantaneous transformation.

A couple years back, I was running a three-day workshop. There was one woman in the class named Margaret, whose ex-husband had left her for a younger girlfriend. Margaret had been

115

struggling with ferocious anger since the split, and had found out a couple weeks previously that the two had moved in together; now she was boiling with anger every day.

When Margaret first practiced this exercise, she changed her anger from a spiky, cold lump of coal in the pit of her stomach to a fluffy pink cloud. When she pulled that cozy little cloud back into her body, she burst into tears.

"Oh my God," she said through her tears, "where did all the anger go?"

This was Saturday afternoon. When she went home that night, her kids told her that her ex and his girlfriend had just gotten engaged. To her own shock and amazement, she didn't feel any anger. She grabbed her phone and sent two texts, one to her ex and one to his new fiancée. Both read, "I just heard the news; congratulations on the engagement! I'm really happy for you two." She even threw in a kissy-face emoji at the end.

Needless to say, Margaret was amazed at her own transformation.

This exercise works for more than just emotions. You can use it to transform the experience you have around particular memories, or even a pattern of internal dialogue.

Below are some of my tips for using submodalities to change different kinds of experiences:

Changing an emotional feeling
- Identify it in your body and pull it out
- Improve the color, noise, movement, smell, sound, and texture
- Put it back in your body

Changing a negative visual memory
- In your mind, turn it into a photo with a picture frame around it

116

- Make the photo black and white, or sepia
- Make the photo fuzzy and blurry
- Move it off away into the distance

Changing a negative auditory memory
- Lower the volume
- Add some white noise or static to any voices
- Change the pitch of any voices
- Add a funny background song, like "Yakety Sax"

Changing an internal dialogue
- Stick out your thumb
- Move your voice to your thumb
- Say it out loud as you hear it, while you move your thumb
- Change your voice to sound like Mickey Mouse, and repeat the same internal dialogue

Day 23

How to Rebuild
Your Confidence and Self-Esteem

After a split, it is completely normal for you to take a hit to your confidence and self-esteem, so if even after the work we've done over the last three weeks, you're still feeling like you have no self-confidence or as though your self-esteem has plummeted, take a deep breath: it's ok.

We all pretty much go through something like this after a breakup. If your ex broke up with you or if you discovered something like cheating that forced you to break up with him or her, it's completely understandable. That creates a poignant sense of rejection, and when human beings feel rejected, it's natural for us to take it personally. When we take rejection personally, our confidence and self-esteem tank.

Even if the split was mutually decided on and was amicable, it's natural for it to still affect your confidence and self-esteem. You were building something, and investing yourself into it, and it didn't work out. That can hit hard, even when it ends with a friendly close.

This is all natural, but that doesn't mean you have to live with it forever. Rebuilding confidence and self-esteem is one of the major desires that my clients come to me with, so I've gathered a collection of tools and strategies for you to use as you build up your self-image again.

You'll notice a few of the suggestions here are particular uses of tools you've already learned—like the flip-it exercise—while most are new techniques that will specifically address confidence and self-esteem.

Write What Your Best Friend Loves About You

When we feel down about ourselves, sometimes the best root back into self-confidence is to see ourselves through someone else's eyes, so pull out your breakthrough journal and list at least three things your best friend loves about you.

Write Down What You're Good At

Focusing on the great parts of yourself is another tried-and-true method to building your self-esteem. When our confidence has taken a hit, we tend to focus entirely on what we don't like about ourselves, so to shift that momentum, ask yourself what you are good at? On a new page in your breakthrough journal, write at least five things you're good at.

Take Control of the Questions You Are Asking Yourself

Just a couple days ago, we looked at the power of language, and I gave you some tools to shift your language for self-empowerment. In fact, you should have some sticky notes scattered throughout your house right now with empowering questions on them.

Confidence and self-esteem are areas where shifting your language will have a massive impact. Many of the negative questions we tend to ask ourselves after a split, like "What's wrong with me?" or "Why don't they love me anymore?" tend to hit right at our self-image. When we ask ourselves that, our brain will start finding reasons—including wildly exaggerated and completely false reasons. Do that enough and you'll whittle away your self confidence completely.

The ongoing language-shifting that you started a couple days ago will rebuild your confidence over time, but in the moments you're feeling really low you can also use questions to give your self-esteem a boost.

In a moment like that, you can ask yourself the questions from strategies one and two here: What does your best friend love about you?" and "What are you good at?" Even just running through them in your head will instantly start to build up your confidence.

You can also bring in the strategies you've learned about challenging your limiting beliefs with evidence. If your low confidence is tied to feeling unattractive, you might ask yourself, "What evidence do I have that people find me attractive as I am right now?" If your low confidence is tied to thinking you always fail, you might ask yourself, "What evidence do I have that that's not true? Where in life am I succeeding?"

Each of us is different, and breakups can affect our self-esteem differently. Wherever it is that you feel particularly down, start asking yourself questions that challenge your negative self-image.

Decide on a Mantra That You Can Repeat to Yourself When You Feel Low in Confidence

Mantras are useful tools to have in your toolbelt as you work on rebuilding your confidence. They allow you to shift your focus in an instant, and the ritual of repeating a mantra—and using the same mantra over days and weeks—strengthens the power of the words.

Pick a mantra that resonates with you; something that feels like it boosts you where you need it. Some possible options include:

- "I can do this"
- "Good things are coming"
- "I accept myself and love myself, just as I am"
- "I am enough, I do enough, I have enough"
- "I'm in charge of my life and my future"

Use the Flip-It Technique to Focus on the Good in Your Situation.

The Flip-It technique, which you learned back on day 10, is a great tool for combating low self-confidence. When you're dealing with poor self-esteem, just flip it and ask yourself: "What's the good in this situation?"

If you're dealing with a particular circumstance that's dredging up low self-esteem—maybe you're trying to start dating again or worrying about parenting on your own—flip-it will shift your focus onto the silver linings of where you find yourself. As you give attention to those positive aspects, your self-image will improve too.

Do Things Differently—Small Change for a Big Impact

If you do things the way you always have, you're going to get the same results. Simply by making small changes, you're showing yourself that you're in a new chapter of your life—and a great chapter at that.

These small changes will do wonders for your self-confidence. Some changes you could take on include:

- Put in some extra time to dress well in the morning.
- Wear your favorite color or an outfit you love.
- Try a new hairstyle.

121

- Start a new exercise routine, especially if you don't yet exercise regularly.
- Change your furniture around or do some redecorating, especially if you're living in a home you used to share with your ex.
- Surround yourself with photos of happy memories.

Face Your Fears

Oftentimes in life, the only way out is through. If there's an area of your life where you're especially lacking confidence, tackle it head-on. Feeling bad about how you look? Start a new exercise regime, read up on healthy eating, or give yourself a wardrobe makeover. Feeling like you're bad at socializing or meeting new people? Find a club you could join that focuses on something you're interested in.

This isn't about making yourself the world's greatest in whatever area you're feeling low confidence in; rather, it's about creating action and tangible results—even small, gradual results—to transform how you think about part of your life.

One client I was working with—Michael—had recently split with an ex. She had often complained that he wouldn't ever help out with cooking meals, and when he did try to cook a dinner for them, she would only criticize the food. When Michael found out she'd started dating a chef, he felt even worse about it all.

I encouraged Michael to learn a few recipes that he could be proud of. He found a few that sounded good and plugged away until he felt comfortable cooking them. Was Michael ever going to become a world-renowned chef? Definitely not, but he *did* know that he could always whip up a meal for a date or friends—and cook something that people would love eating—and that made a huge difference in his whole self-image.

Oftentimes, it only takes a small improvement to jump-start your self-confidence.

Create Mind Movies

Visualization is a powerful tool—and a great one for building confidence and self-esteem. When you're lacking confidence about a particular situation, take a few minutes to create a mind movie. Imagine yourself in that situation, but full of confidence and capability.

Nervous before a date? Create a mind movie about the date going great, with you putting your best foot forward. Feeling self-conscious about going to the beach in your swimsuit? Create a mind movie of you strutting your stuff on the sand, with heads turning to you because you look so great.

When you create a mind movie, you are not only showing yourself that it *is* possible for you to be confident—you're also creating new mental patterns. Remember, your brain doesn't really know the difference between what's real and what's imaginary. When you envision yourself acting and speaking confidently, you're literally creating new muscle memory, even though it's all in your head!

Act as If

Not *feeling* confident? That's ok. Challenge yourself to walk and talk as if you *were* 100% confident in yourself. Ever hear the phrase, "Fake it till you make it"? That's pretty much the idea here.

Acting as if you're confident has three great effects: Firstly, you get the practice of acting and speaking with confidence, even though at first it's just acting; the more you practice, the more natural it becomes. Secondly, you start hitting the physiology of changing your mood—remember, even just changing your body language will have immediate impacts on your state of mind. And thirdly, when you act as if you have confidence, the world will start responding to you on those terms. People will respond to you as if you had great self-confidence, which means they'll respond positively to you, and that response will build your true self-image and self-esteem.

Day 24

Rediscovering Your
Identity and Values

When you're in a relationship, it's natural for you to take on some of your partner's values and interests. You might start going out to places they like to eat, or going hiking because it's something they love. You might get into classic movies with them or listen to more of the music they like. As you start to build a life together, you start to adopt each other's dreams and values as well.

Again, this is all a natural part of relationships. We're interested in someone, so we become interested in the things they like. The more two people are together, the more they tend to blend their wishes, values, and goals, but then when the relationship splits apart, we're left in limbo. We've built up a huge part of our identity around this other person, and then that person is gone, so who are we now?

A pivotal point in turning breakup into breakthrough is rediscovering your own identity—who *you* are, what you value, and what you love.

I once worked with a client by the name of Marcie. Marcie was telling me how it had become difficult for her to enjoy watching *Top Gear*, a popular show all about cars; Marcie and her ex, Wes, had always watched it together. It was one of their things, but now that they'd broken up, anytime Marcie sat down to watch it, she just felt sad, angry, frustrated, and alone.

I asked Marcie what it was she liked about *Top Gear* and her brow furrowed while she thought about it for a few seconds.

"You know," she said, "I'm not really sure. Honestly, the show kind of annoys me. I'm not that into cars, and one of the hosts really gets on my nerves."

Marcie paused in thought for another few seconds.

"Actually," she exclaimed, "I don't think I really even like the show at all!"

As we talked more about it, Marcie realized that she had loved watching *Top Gear* because of how much Wes had loved it. They would get to spend quality time together, joke about the show together, and it made Marcie happy to see how excited Wes was about sharing it with her. She wasn't wild about the show itself, but she enjoyed it for the role it played in their relationship and how it helped her connect with Wes.

Marcie laughed to realize that now that Wes was gone, she had no reason to watch the show anymore. It was time for her to rediscover and refocus on her own interests; what lit *her* up.

Rediscovering Your Identity Through Your Values

Defining your values—the qualities of life you seek out most— is a great way to rediscover and focus on your own identity.

In a moment, I'm going to walk you through an exercise on discovering and defining your values; for now, we're going to focus on your values in the context of a relationship—both because it will help provide clarity on your past relationship, and because it will help you move forward into future relationships. This same exercise can be applied to your values in your career, your social life, your finances, even your life as a whole, but it's useful to practice first with a concrete, specific view, so we're going to start with relationships.

So, you know the drill—turn to a new page in your breakthrough journal.

Write a list of all of the things you value in a relationship; things that are important to you to have in a relationship. Focus on broad descriptive qualities, like "adventure" instead of "going on an exotic trip around the world together."

Some values you might put on your list include:

- Passion
- Fun
- Trust
- Honesty
- Love
- Adventure

- Happiness
- Security
- Excitement
- Humor
- Loyalty
- Freedom

This is by no means a comprehensive list of every possible value, but it should help get you started.

Once you have that list written, circle your top five values. If you could only have five of these values in your next relationship, which would you choose? Now, we're going to get even more specific. Of those five, if you could only have *one*, which would it be? Write that value at the top of a new page.

If you could have one *more* of the remaining 4, which would you choose? Write that one underneath the first. Continue through each of your top five until you have them ranked in order of importance to you.

Now, dig deeper into these values and define what they really mean to you. Having adventure in a relationship might be a top value for you and another person, but it could mean very different things to the two of you and look completely different in a relationship.

In your breakthrough journal, write answers to the following questions, for each of your top five values:

- What does this value mean to you, in the context of a relationship?
- How do you know when you have it?

You might find yourself rediscovering parts of yourself you've long known, or you might be surprised by what comes up in this exercise. It's important to remember that our values tend to change and evolve over time. What you value in a relationship in your fifties might not be the same as what you valued most in your twenties. Circumstances can change our values too; maybe you've discovered a love of adventure and now want more of that, or maybe after an unfaithful partner you've come to value trust more.

Of course, there is no right or wrong answer here. What matters is that you're clear on *your* values and what they mean to you. Tomorrow we'll start focusing on getting you back into the world of dating and romance, and the values you've defined here will be vital in creating the love life you deserve.

Day 25

Lessons for Loving Again

As we turn our attention to creating the amazing future of your dreams, it's time to start talking about strategies that will set you up to win as you re-enter the dating world.

There are two common pitfalls that you want to keep an eye out for from the outset. The first is the forever-not-ready pitfall. If you're just a few weeks or a month out of a decades-long relationship, it's totally understandable for you to want to take some time before dating again. There is no clear-cut answer as to when you're ready again, and there's no universal truth about how long it *should* take. Different people have different journeys; you just have to be true to yourself.

There is sometimes a temptation, however, to forever tell yourself that you're just not ready yet. I worked with a client once who told me that she wasn't yet ready to date again—and it had been over four years! This can be a tempting trap because, deep down, we're just afraid of getting hurt again, or we're refusing to actually let go of the past relationship.

If your mindset now is that you want to wait longer before dating, only you can tell if that's your best choice, but be sure you're looking within and are clear that you aren't just avoiding dating out of fear, or secretly hanging onto your past relationship.

The second pitfall is sort of the flipside of the first— scrambling for a replacement. Sometimes after a painful split, we

129

can be tempted to immediately find a replacement; not just someone new to date, but someone who will fill all the painful gaps of the lost relationship; someone to make everything better. In this danger zone, people tend to become wildly infatuated with the first person that shows any interest in them, and then want to leap immediately into a relationship that's just as serious as their last. This never works out well.

I worked with one client named Harold, who fell into this pitfall. Soon after Harold had split from his wife, he took himself on a vacation to start living again and focusing on his happiness— great so far—but on this vacation, he met a woman named Jessica, who started showing him some affection. Harold was so desperate to feel any sort of love and affection again that he dove head-over-heels into a new relationship. Jessica was wrong for Harold, though, in just about every conceivable way. She was controlling, manipulative, demanding, and before long, Harold was even more miserable than he was before.

Because Harold just leapt into the comfort of a familiar sort of relationship, he found himself taking one step forward and two steps back, and it took him months to realize it and move on from his rebound relationship.

If it's soon after your split and you're feeling desperate for a new relationship, you might be in this pitfall. Before you jump into anything serious, make sure you have a clear head and realistic expectations.

And don't worry—the strategies and insights I'll be sharing with you over the next few days are going to help you avoid both of these pitfalls, so you can re-enter the dating world empowered and ready for success.

Getting Clear on What You're Looking For

Before you dive back into the ocean of dating, you need to be clear on what you're looking for.

When it comes to dating, there's Mr. or Ms. Right, and then there's Mr. or Ms. Right Now. The former are the people in which you see potential for a long-term relationship; someone you might settle down with one day. The latter are the people who don't necessarily hold much long-term potential for you but would be fun to date for a bit and just have some fun with.

First, let's be clear—it's totally fine to be looking for either or open to both. If you're not yet feeling ready to start something serious, that's completely fine. It's ok to just let yourself have some fun and enjoy the dating process. On the other hand, you might feel like you're not really interested in dating around casually, but are only interested in dating people to find a long-term partner. That's completely fine too.

You might feel like you're open to either—ready to explore a relationship if you come across a Mr. or Ms. Right, but also fine with just having fun with a Mr. or Ms. Right Now.

As with so much in life, there is no right or wrong answer. There's only what's right for *you* here and now, and only you know the answer to that.

Being Realistic About Romance

When most of us think about ideal partners, we tend to think of a person who is going to match our every want and need. It'll be the person we have the most fun with, talk about our deepest desires with, get the best advice from about troubles we're having, be the one we gossip to about work—he or she will be our everything, but is that actually realistic?

Let's think about friendships for a moment. I've got one friend, Janice, who is an absolute blast to go out with for a night on the town. She's a wild child through and through, and I know a night out with her will have us dancing and bar-hopping till the sun peaks up in the morning. It'll be a great time, even if I only go out with her once every few months; then I need a week to recover!

But is Janice the friend I go to when I need career advice, or want to have deep conversations with about family troubles? Definitely not.

I've got another friend, Grace. Grace is a single mom, and we often meet up for coffee in the afternoon. She's the friend I go to for parenting advice, or just to laugh and connect with about our everyday lives. She's kind, wise, and supportive. But would I call Grace up for an impromptu cruise vacation? Nope!

With our friendships, we tend to naturally accept that different people will play different roles in our lives. We don't expect any of our friends to be our *one* friend who meets all our needs, but when it comes to romance, we do expect that, and it's just not realistic. Your partner is going to be *all* things to you, but he or she is not going to fulfill every last one of your social needs. When we expect that, we only set ourselves up for disappointment and frustration.

When you start thinking about new partners—either Mr. or Ms. Right or Mr. or Ms. Right Now—it's vital that you bring this romantic realism with you. There may be some roles that you *do* need a romantic partner to play in your life—and tomorrow we'll uncover them when you design your ideal partner—but you've got to remember that even your ideal partner won't fill every role, and that's ok.

Starting to Date Again

It can sometimes feel daunting to start dating again, but luckily things are easier today than they ever have been.

I'm a big fan of using online dating apps or websites if you're feeling hesitant about dating again. Online dating provides a great opportunity to ease back into things, all from the comfort of your own home. You can be on the couch in your pajamas and start swiping to make new connections. Online dating allows you to chat with new people and get back out there, without the pressure of actually having to meet up in person—unless you decide you want to, of course. If you've been out of the dating world for a while, online dating can be a great way to stretch those muscles again and get back in the swing of things.

If you do decide to use an online dating app or website, there are some guidelines you'll want to follow:

- Have a profile that reflects your true personality
- Keep it light
- Don't give away any personal details
- Always use photos that reflect the perception you want to create; how you present yourself is going to reflect the people who want to connect with you.
- Be honest
- If you decide you want to meet in person, be safe and arrange to meet somewhere with plenty of people. Let your friends know where you are

Whether you're jumping into online dating or out-in-the-world matchmaking, here are some do's and don'ts to keep in mind.

Dating Do's

- Let your friends know that you're ready to date again
- Meet for a coffee first rather than dinner
- Be open-minded about meeting different types of people than you've dated in the past, to help you discover what you really like
- Smile!
- Ask questions about your date to find out who they are
- Leave when you want to
- Be realistic and take off the rose-tinted glasses

Dating Don'ts

- Talk about your ex
- Discuss your sad story
- Talk about yourself all night
- Jump straight into another relationship
- Look to them to save you
- Exaggerate or tell untruths – if things develop further, they're going to come out eventually
- Overstep your own boundaries
- Bombard them with text messages or calls after the date

Day 26

Designing Your Ideal Partner

Yesterday, I told you what we'll be up to today, and this is one area that people tend to have a lot of fun with—designing your ideal partner.

As you think about dating again, it's important for you to have a clear idea of what you want in your next partner. For one, we have a tendency to notice what we focus on. The clearer you are on what you're looking for, the more likely you are to spot them. Also, you'll be better prepared to spot red flags in potential partners.

Even if you're not yet jumping back into the dating world, this is still an important exercise for you to take on now. Not only will it help get you thinking and focusing more on the future, it will also help you more clearly understand what didn't work in your past relationship, as I'll show you at the end of this chapter.

Designing Your Ideal Partner

On a new page in your breakthrough journal, brainstorm and list out all of the attributes that you would ideally like in a partner. This can be a mixture of both wants and needs. Be sure to state them all in the positive—for example, "supportive" instead of "not super critical," or "good with kids" instead of "doesn't hate kids."

Be sure to cover all the areas that are important to you in a relationship, including:

- looks
- personality traits
- values
- interests and hobbies
- education or career
- humor
- family
- finances

Next, identify up to five must-not-haves—these are traits that would be an absolute deal-breaker for you—red flags that this person is definitely not a potential long-term partner. Maybe they would compromise your values, like "lies" or "is emotionally distant," or maybe they're just something you really couldn't deal with in a partner, like "smokes" or "doesn't want kids." Remember, there's no right or wrong answer—just what would be a deal-breaker for *you*. List these must-not-haves—up to five—in your breakthrough journal now.

With this outline, you've given yourself a solid foundation for dating again. When it comes to the must-not-haves, it's important that you stay true to them when it comes to long-term potential. Remember, if you sacrifice your own values or boundaries, you're only going to end up hurting yourself.

If you do encounter a must-not-have in someone you're interested in, it's up to you what you do at that point. They don't have long-term potential, so they're definitely not Mr. or Ms. Right, but maybe they still qualify as a Mr. or Ms. Right Now. Then again, maybe not. Maybe they're someone you'd like to have as just a friend, or maybe not. What's important is that you make decisions from an informed place and that you can know you're being true to your values and boundaries. This exercise acts as a safety net for you so that you can start to date with more confidence and less fear of getting your heart broken. Dating again is a great way to boost your self-esteem and move forward past your split, and this safety net ensures that you don't trip yourself up along the way.

Checking Your Ex

Remember how I said that you can also use this exercise to help you understand why things didn't work out with your ex?

On a new page, I want you to write out all the wants and needs that you listed which your ex did *not* meet. If you listed "outgoing and social" as a trait of your ideal partner, and your ex was anything but that, you'll write that in your new list.

Next, I want you to write down any of the must-not-haves that your ex *did* have. Maybe "lies" was one of your deal-breakers, but your ex was carrying on an affair behind your back.

This new list is an illustration of how your ex differed from your ideal partner—and you might be surprised to see just how far off the mark he or she was!

Day 27

Getting Excited About Life Again

When we're in the thick weeds of a breakup, it can feel impossible to be excited about life or even to see through to anything other than the pain of the split, but now that you've gone through over three weeks of transformation and breakthrough-healing, it's time for you to begin designing the compelling future you're living into.

Remember that one of the four keys to surviving and thriving is focusing on the future, and today we're going to launch into that full-force.

Your bright future isn't just about future relationships and romance. With the tools and strategies you've been learning these recent weeks, you're ready to create a future full of possibilities in every area of life.

Yesterday, you designed an ideal partner; the dream of everything you'd want and need in a future love. Today, we'll broaden that scope so you can put down on paper the dreams you have for your life as a whole. To do that, you're going to create your dream breakup bucket list.

In your breakthrough journal, write all the things you want to do in life that you never thought you'd be able to, or that you dream of but just haven't gotten around to yet. The fresh start that you're in after your split is a space of limitless possibilities and wide-open potential, so now is the perfect time to refocus on your dreams and life goals, and then start moving towards them.

As you create your list, put down anything that comes to mind, big or small. Maybe you always wanted to travel to another continent, but your ex just wasn't wild about travel. Maybe you wanted to get a tattoo, but your ex always looked down on the idea. Maybe there's a pair of shoes you've had your eye on, but your ex didn't think they were worth putting into the budget.

All those dreams and goals and desires, big and small—take some time now to write them in your breakthrough journal.

Your breakup bucket list will focus your energy on the future that you want to create and can have a surprisingly profound impact, not only on your thoughts and activities, but also on the healing process of moving past your relationship.

I once worked with a client named Carl, a middle-aged man whose wife of decades had recently left him. When I had Carl write out his bucket list, he somewhat sheepishly put down that he wanted to climb Everest. He'd always dreamed of it, but his ex-wife had always put her foot down about it, thinking it was just too dangerous and expensive.

Now, at this point in his life, Carl was a bit past the age that most people would be to give Everest a shot, but his children were all adults now and his ex wasn't around to argue against the idea, so Carl figured he'd just go for it.

He did some research and discovered that there was a group in the area that was working towards an Everest expedition. The group was aiming to make an Everest attempt in just eight or nine months, and it seemed a bit of a stretch that Carl could get himself ready in that time, but he decided to just go for it anyway.

Carl started going on training hikes and climbs with the group, which got him out of the house and active again. He loved it, but on top of that, he also found out the group would meet up for a few drinks on Friday evenings, and Carl started going out for those as well. He clicked with the group both on and off the mountain, and he found his social calendar filling up again.

One day, Carl came in for a session and, with a somewhat mystified smile on his face, said, "You know, Sara, I haven't even had the time to stress out about the divorce these last few weeks. I've been out climbing and training and hanging out with these new folks. I've been having too much fun to be depressed about things."

That's the power of a breakup bucket list. When you start pursuing your dreams, whether big or small, you'll find that the positive momentum in your life builds. Before you know it, your life is too full of passion, fun, and fulfillment for you to even have time to worry about your split.

Day 28

Building Up Your Wheel of Life

As we continue our focus on designing and activating your amazing future, I'm going to introduce you to one of the most indispensable tools for evaluating and forwarding the diverse areas of your life—the wheel of life.

As you can see below, the wheel of life is divided up into 10 segments. Each of these segments represents a distinct area of your life, and taken together, they comprise all of what goes into a balanced, healthy life. In your breakthrough journal, draw out a copy of the wheel of life and its 10 segments.

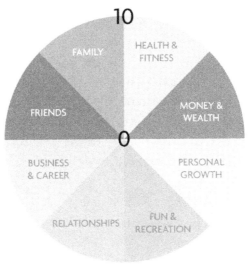

The concept was originally created by
Paul J. Meyer, founder of Success Motivation® Institute, Inc.

What you'll do next is self-evaluate where you are in your life right now, in terms of fulfillment, in each of these 10 categories on a scale from zero to 10. Zero here indicates being completely unfulfilled in that area, while 10 represents being 100% fulfilled. Obviously, it's a bit of a personal judgment call to give each of these categories a quantified number, but do your best to be radically honest with where you are.

For each number, make a mark in the middle of the appropriate wedge, at a corresponding distance from the center of the wheel—the middle of the wheel representing zero, the outer rim representing 10.

For example, if in fun and recreation, you're currently at a five out of 10, you'd make a mark in that wedge halfway from the center of the wheel to the outer rim. If you're currently at a full 10 out of 10, you'd make a mark right on the outer rim, and so on.

Once you've ranked and marked each of these 10 categories, connect the dots to form your current inner wheel; it'll probably look somewhere between a lopsided circle and a lumpy star.

Now, we're going to look forward into the future—three months into the future, to be precise. For each category, ask yourself where on the same scale from zero to 10 you would like to be in three months.

Choose a goal for each category that is going to push you but is realistic. Maybe you've ranked your fulfillment in health and fitness currently as a two out of 10. Would it be realistic to think you're going to rocket up to a 10 out of 10 in just a few months? Probably not, but maybe a three-month goal of hitting 5 out of 10 is more reasonable.

For each category, make a new mark on the appropriate wedge—in a different color this time—then connect those goal-marks to create a future inner wheel.

These numbers help quantify things and guide your thinking, but we, of course, want to get more specific with what these transformations in your life are going to look like. In your breakthrough journal, write any and all specific goals that will accomplish the movement you've committed to.

Let's say you're currently at a two out of 10 in health and fitness, and your three-month goal is to reach a 5 out of 10. Your specific goals to accomplish that movement might include things like, "Implement an exercise routine of going to the gym at least three times per week," or "Talk to a nutritionist and create a new nutrition plan." You want these goals to be specific and measurable; something that will be clear when you accomplish it.

You'll be amazed at how working on one area of the wheel of life affects other areas as well. At one recent retreat, I worked with a woman named Courtney who was in a situation like what I described above—she ranked herself at a two out of 10 in health and fitness and committed to taking herself to a 5 out of 10 over the following three months.

Courtney put together her plan to make that shift. Her plan included cutting back on alcohol, starting to work with a personal trainer, and taking Zumba classes. Over the next couple months, Courtney put the plan into action, and not surprisingly, her health and fitness did improve, but more than that, she made new friends at her Zumba class, and her social life started filling up again with fun outings. Because she was losing weight and feeling better in her body, her confidence jumped up and she began dating again— something she'd been reticent to do before. Because her mind was clearer, thanks to her healthy body and lifestyle, she started making better decisions with her legal team regarding the divorce. Just by focusing on transforming one area of her wheel of life that needed attention, Courtney transformed her whole life.

Now that you have *your* list of goals—the ways you're going to increase your standing on the wheel of life—you get to start creating an action plan to accomplish them, and we've already worked on a tool to put goals into actionable steps. It's time for some stepping stones.

For each goal, write out the first three stepping stones action steps, and give yourself a deadline why which you'll commit to having the first step in each goal completed.

All of this is going to entail a fair bit of writing and planning, but will prove so worth it; this is your launch-pad for a compelling future, and the more focus and thought you invest in it now, the more you'll get out of it. Your future is worth it, so dive in.

Day 29

How to Create a Compelling Future

As we near the finish line of our 30-day journey together, you have a tool-belt full of strategies and techniques for turning your breakup into breakthroughs—breakthroughs in every area of your life.

With yesterday's exercise of committing to new goals and action steps to expand your wheel of life, you have a clear direction ahead of you, so today, we're going to focus on launching into those goals in a way that sets you up for continued success.

Don't Keep Your Commitments to Yourself

At this point, you know well that transforming your life isn't a single-player game. From way back on day seven, you've had the foundation of your breakup support team aiding you on your journey.

With the new goals you've laid out for yourself, it's again time to bring others in, by sharing the journey you're committing to.

When you make a commitment to yourself and don't tell anyone about it, it can be all too easy to let things start to slip, piece by piece. If you've ever broken a secret New Year's Resolution by the end of January, you know what I'm talking about here.

When we share our commitments with others, we create a new level of accountability with ourselves. We've put skin in the game by giving our word to others, and even that unspoken social expectation can sometimes be all we need to stay the course towards our dreams.

Beyond that, when you share with friends and family the new goals and new path that you're committing to, they're going to want to be there for you to help however they can.

In my years of working in this field, I've actually had the pleasure of attending more than a few divorce parties thrown by my clients. Contrary to what people tend to think when they first hear the term, these get-togethers are always a beautiful celebration of individuals beginning a new chapter in their lives, thanking and recognizing their friends and family for all of their support, and most importantly, sharing their commitments for what's next. Some divorce parties I've attended were just an intimate gathering of a dozen people or less, while others were closer to a packed nightclub, but in all of them, a pivotal step for these people was sharing their new goals with the people they loved.

Of course, a divorce party might not be quite your style. In any case, I can't stress enough how valuable it will be for you to start sharing your new commitments with others. Your breakup support team is a great place to start.

Creating a Vision Board

Another tool for creating momentum behind your new vision for your future is to create a vision board.

You may have made a vision board before; if not, you're probably familiar with the concept. The idea is to create an illustrative collage that encapsulates the new vision of your life you're creating. Gather together pictures, photos, cutouts from magazines, words or phrases—any visual representation that speaks of the new life that you're living towards. There's no right or wrong way to create a vision board; you want to design it so that it speaks most deeply to *you* and inspires you when you see it.

Vision boards have a funny way of becoming shockingly prescient. A couple years ago, I was moving into a new house, and while unpacking boxes, I came across one of the first vision boards I ever created. I had made it back in my early twenties and hadn't looked at it or even thought about it in years. I pulled it out to look over it for a trip down memory lane, and I was shocked. A big focus of the vision board was the dream I had for the house I wanted to live in one day—and the house on my vision board was almost an exact twin of the house into which I was moving. From the exterior of the house, to the neighborhood, even to the layout inside, my new home was almost an exact manifestation of the house I'd envisioned years ago.

When you create your new vision board, of course you won't be packing it away. Hang it up somewhere in your home where you'll see it regularly as you go throughout your day. The illustration of your dreams coming to fruition will keep you inspired and focused on bringing to life everything you're striving towards.

Day 30

Keeping Your Momentum Alive

We've come now to our final day of this 30-day journey together. Over the last month, you've learned and practiced dozens of tools, strategies, and techniques for creating breakthroughs and personal transformation through the crisis of your split, and you've been applying and practicing them in your life.

I want to take a moment to acknowledge you for all you've put in. I know from my own experience and my work with hundreds of clients just how difficult this journey can be at points. It gets painful, it gets messy, it gets hard. Sometimes you just want to throw your hands up and give up, but you stuck with it and living that commitment makes all the difference. Way back on day one, you gave your word to play full-out, and you have. Congratulations for all you've put in, and for the stand you've taken for the life you deserve.

Assessing Anew

In our first week together, you took an inventory of where you were in your journey—what you were experiencing and feeling, the circumstances you were in, and so on.

As we complete this month-long journey, it's important to take time to reassess where you are now, both to recognize and celebrate the progress that you've made, and to look forward into the future to see where you get to go from here.

Turn to a new page in your breakthrough journal, write your current view of your breakup, and the opportunities it has opened up for you. Take at least five minutes to write this and let your focus go wherever it wants to go.

After you've done that, take a moment to read over it again, and think back to where your mindset and perspectives were at the start of this journey when you first picked up the book. On a new page, answer the following questions:

- How has your view of your breakup evolved and changed over the last month?
- What opportunities are you aware of now that you weren't seeing one month ago?

Next, we're going to do a reassessment of your emotional experiences. On day four, you listed all the words that described your feelings and emotions about your breakup (words like angry, hurt, excited, optimistic, and so on). Now, you're going to go through this exercise again.

On a new page, take a few minutes to write all the words that describe how you are now feeling about your breakup and the road ahead. Once you've done that, I want you to look over that list and circle the words that feel most prominent and powerful for you right now, maybe three to six of them.

Take a look at how intensely you're feeling particular emotions on a scale of one to 10—with one being the least intense and 10 being the most intense. In your breakthrough journal, record the intensity of the following emotions for you right now:

- Anger
- Sadness
- Panic
- Fear

149

- Happiness
- Optimism
- Excitement

If any of the feelings you circled from your list a moment ago are *not* among the seven emotions above, copy those down and rank how intensely you're feeling those as well, on a scale from one to 10.

Now, it's time to look more specifically at the progress you've made. Turn back in your breakthrough journal, all the way to the work you did on day four. Look at the one-to-10 rankings of your emotions from day four and compare them to the ones you just created.

On a new page in your breakthrough journal, reflect on these changes and answer the following questions:

1. What differences do you see between these two assessments?
2. Which emotions have you increased, and which have you decreased?
3. How are the changes in these emotional states manifesting themselves in your life now?
4. As you move forward, where do you want to further increase or decrease your emotions and states of mind? This may include some emotions or experiences other than the ones you've listed and ranked from one to 10.

Keeping the Momentum Alive

Although we're at the end of our month together in this book, your journey of creating the life of your dream lives on, and we want you to keep all the momentum you've created this month.

As you move forward, continue to use the tools, strategies, and techniques you've learned in these pages. I've been involved in this work for years and still use this stuff regularly. Remember, everything here isn't just applicable to processing and moving past a breakup—these are tools for breakthrough-living in every area of your life.

I'm also here and available to you as you continue this journey. You can connect with me in some of the following ways.

For daily tips and advice, you can follow me on:

- Facebook at SaraDavisonDivorceCoaching
- Twitter at @SDDivorceCoach
- Instagram at saradavisondivorcecoach
- LinkedIn at Sara Davison
- Download my FREE Breakup Survival Guide at www.saradavison.com

For further support and coaching, you can:

- Work with me one-on-one, either in-person at my clinic or over Skype
- Learn to become an Accredited Breakup and Divorce Coach Practitioner
- Download my Video Coaching Programs at www.saradavison.com
- Read my other books, available at bookstores and on Amazon
- Attend my workshops, retreats, or speaking events

You can also always email me at sara@saradavison.com.

Keep your commitment to yourself alive and keep turning your dreams into your reality—you've got this!

With love and hugs,

Sara

Glossary

Aggressively Severing: An acrimonious break-up involving conflict with your ex.

Boomerang Effect: This is how you learn to bounce back faster each time you get knocked down emotionally. It gets easier each time to dust yourself down, get back up and put a smile on your face.

'Build On You' Time: This is a period of time that you spend focusing on your personal development and working to create a better future for yourself. It could be working on improving the way you are coping with your situation, learning new skills or creating new experiences for yourself.

Cyber Stalking/Social-media Self-Harming: Following your ex and their friends on social media can cause a lot of pain and heartache. Seeing them getting on with life without you and seemingly enjoying post break-up life will make you feel even worse. It's a good idea to delete all social media ties so that you can't be tempted to log on when you are feeling vulnerable. I know it can feel like a huge wrench to let this voyeuristic contact go, but it will give you a huge sense of relief as soon as you hit that 'unfriend' button.

Detox Your Ex: A technique for getting over your ex, which involves no contact, no social-media contact and no talking about your story or mentioning your ex's name. It will give you more control over your emotions.

Energy Vampires: These are people who drain you of energy when you spend time with them. It feels as if they suck the life out of you, and you feel worse having been around them than you did before. They make you feel uncomfortable and ill at ease in their presence.

Flip-It: Finding the good in any situation, however bad, and focusing on it.

Functionally Friendly: Being able to be amicable with your ex when you are co-parenting. This is the best way to put the children first, to be able to have a friendly conversation and attend school functions together if needed. It is achieved by genuinely focusing on your ex's positive attributes and setting aside any issues there may be between you while you are with the children. This does not mean that you have become good friends or even forgiven what has happened, but it provides a workable relationship, which is in the best interests of your children.

Hamster Wheel Questions: A thought process or action where you are chasing your tail asking questions that you will never be able to answer. You will end up going around in circles and never make any progress forward. It is a destructive mindset and stops you from healing and moving on.

Healing Cycle Process: These are the different stages of emotion that you will go through after your break-up. It is based on the Loss Cycle by Kübler-Ross.

Light Bulb Moment: This is when you suddenly realize something that gives you immediate clarity about a situation

Mind Movie: This is a technique that helps you to prepare for situations you are worried about. Imagine the scenario in your mind, and run it like a movie at the cinema. See you reacting well and being strong, hear what you are saying and feel how good it feels to be in control. Imagine it all going well and being pleased at how it has worked out.

Mr./Mrs. Right Now: Not everyone you meet after your break-up will have the potential to be Mr. or Mrs. Right, but that doesn't mean you should stop dating. Mr./Mrs. Right Now is the perfect person for you at the time.

Shoe Shifting: Stepping into someone else's shoes and seeing a particular situation through their eyes. It involves you taking into account their background, their education, their thought processes, opinions and beliefs so that you see their map of the world and gain a deeper understanding of why they are acting or reacting in certain ways. This is a powerful technique that provides increased clarity and helps you to understand their behavior, particularly if their actions are hurting you.

SSS System: Step up, suck it up and sort it out. The way to use this is to imagine that you have no other option or choice other than coping with your current dilemma. See yourself being strong and step into that persona; breathe in deeply and imagine that you are gaining strength from your breathing. Ask the new, stronger you what is one small thing you can do right now to make it better. In this positive state you will find better answers that will help you to move forward.

Stepping Stones: These are tiny steps that you write in your Action Plan that help you to keep moving forward after your break-up.

Stuffing Your Emotions: Not allowing yourself to feel any negative emotions.

Switch-Flicking Moment: When you get to a certain point and your emotions change so that you can never feel the same way again. The trick is to use this positively to park the dark thoughts and see what is ahead.

Teflon Suit: Letting things wash over you like water off a duck's back. This is a technique to protect you from getting hurt emotionally, which enables you to stay calm and balanced.

About the Author

Sara Davison, best known as 'The Divorce Coach' is the UK's most sought-after authority on break-up, separation and divorce. Revolutionizing the way we view and navigate one of life's most traumatic events, Sara's quest to banish the stigma surrounding divorce and prove that the end of a relationship can be the most empowering, life-affirming event to ever happen to you, is fast catching-on.

Sara is also the author of best-selling book, *Uncoupling*, and created and launched the UK's first ever Break-Up Recovery Retreats dubbed "Heartbreak Hotel". She has been invited by Ministry of Justice to advise on reforming divorce laws in the UK. Sara is also the Patron of The Dash Charity which supports women, children and men coping with all kinds of domestic abuse.

Sara's coaching programs equip both men and women with the tools and techniques needed to regain control of their lives and feel happy again after their breakup. She works with a wide range of clients including celebrities, stay at home mums and business professionals. An NLP Master Practitioner and qualified hypnotherapist, Sara combines 20 years' coaching experience together with her own personal experience of marriage breakdown to create bespoke coaching programs designed to help individuals transition through the turbulent terrain of breakups and reclaim their lives as stronger, happier versions of themselves.

In 2018 Sara launched her "Online Break-Up and Divorce Coach Practitioner Accreditation Program" training people how to become a Coach. She shares her coaching techniques and business strategies to enable them to help clients navigate their break-ups and grow a global coaching business.

A certified motivational speaker and regular media commentator and contributor, Sara has worked and trained with the most revered experts in the field of personal development including Anthony Robbins, Paul McKenna, Richard Bandler, Michael Neill and the Barefoot Doctor. Sara was inspired to create her bespoke coaching programs after feeling helpless and frustrated by the lack of practical and emotional support when experiencing the breakdown of her own marriage. Her empathetic and holistic approach has cornered a gap in the marketplace and helped dozens of people across the world rebuild their lives for the better.

Sara said: "Nothing prepared me for the breakdown of my marriage and, after struggling to find any effective or practical support during that two-year period, I felt passionate about channeling all I had learnt to try and help others. My business and holistic background and qualifications enabled me to create strategies and step by step guides that traverse the practical as well as the emotional challenges. I believe that my coaching is the missing piece to the information available in the market today. It's everything I wish I'd had access to during my own divorce."

Sara works with clients from all over the world at all stages of their break-up journeys, from the first tremors of doubt through to twenty years post break-up when people can still be trapped in destructive cyclical patterns. The format of her coaching programmes vary to suit the needs of the individual, from one-on-one private coaching to the immersive group environment of a workshop on the Break-Up Recovery Retreats and Break-Up

Breakthrough video coaching programme, which can be completed at home. Full details can be found at www.saradavison.com.

Sara is passionate about showing people how break-ups can be the start of a new exciting phase of your life. She walks her talk and is living proof that it is possible to turn your life around. Sara is happily divorced and a single mum to her 10-year-old son and lives with him near London, UK.

Printed in Great Britain
by Amazon

24924301R00096